'What a fantastic resource for all who are concerned with parenting, teaching and supporting children who have experienced developmental trauma. As the title suggests, Christine Gordon explains so articulately and thoroughly why children who have been harmed in their early years can be very challenging to parent, how the children feel about themselves, how they experience relationships and the world about them, how to support their "healing" through developmental reparenting. The uniqueness and innovation in this resource is in the practical nature of connecting executive functioning difficulties – the "why does my child do this?" – to the "what can I do?" and "what can I say?"

Packed full of ideas, suggestions and resources for strategies and interventions, all clearly written by Christine, and wonderfully illustrated by Corinne Watt, this book is not to be missed – highly recommended.'

Edwina Grant, Chair of Scottish Attachment In Action

'This book will be of great help to adults who care for children with developmental trauma. Christine Gordon deftly helps to close the gap between understanding these children and knowing what to do to provide the consistently compassionate care they need to recover from the effects of early life trauma.'

Jonathan Baylin, PhD, co-author with Daniel Hughes of
The Neurobiology of Attachment-focused Therapy

Parenting Strategies to Help Adopted and Fostered Children with Their Behaviour

Parenting Strategies to Help Adopted and Fostered Children with Their Behaviour

Trauma-Informed Guidance and Action Charts

Christine Gordon
Illustrations by Corinne Watt

Jessica Kingsley *Publishers*
London and Philadelphia

First published in 2018
by Jessica Kingsley Publishers
73 Collier Street
London N1 9BE, UK
and
400 Market Street, Suite 400
Philadelphia, PA 19106, USA

www.jkp.com

Library of Congress Cataloging in Publication Data
A CIP catalog record for this book is available from the Library of Congress

British Library Cataloguing in Publication Data
A CIP catalogue record for this book is available from the British Library

ISBN 978 1 78592 386 9
eISBN 978 1 78450 738 1

Printed and bound in the United States

The accompanying PDF can be downloaded from www.jkp.com/voucher using the code GORDONPARENT

This book is dedicated to all the parents we have worked with at ADAPT Scotland. Your commitment to your children and willingness to embrace the principles of developmental reparenting have not only provided the best environment for your children to thrive, but have also given me the opportunity to 'practise' the ideas that are the central focus of this book. I thank each and every one of you for allowing me to do this.

Christine Gordon

Contents

Part 2: Action Charts

Preface

The aim of this book is to help parents, carers and teachers understand the profound impact of pre- and post-birth toxic environments. The impact of exposure to drugs and alcohol or to the stress of domestic violence in the womb, birth trauma, neglect, physical and sexual abuse and multiple separations, singly or in combination, have been widely researched and documented. This research highlights the impairment to children's psychological, neurological and physiological development of living in these environments. This book explores why these early experiences can continue to impact children after babyhood and when they are placed in safe and stable family environments.

This book also aims to help parents, carers and teachers find ways to move beyond understanding why children act in the way they do to what they can do to actively address the behavioural issues that traumatized children often display.

The book is divided into two parts: the first focuses on the 'why' of the behavioural difficulties many traumatized children display, the second part comprises charts that outline the 'why' of specific behavioural challenges, alongside what you can do to address these issues. If you are struggling with particular behaviours you might want to move straight to the charts. That is fine. This is not a book that needs to be read in a linear fashion. Use it in the way that is most helpful to you. However, I hope that the charts will inspire you to read the more detailed analysis contained in part one to deepen your understanding of the 'why' and help you to develop your own 'what charts' that are more reflective of you and your children. For this reason, I have included a blank chart in the book. Please feel free to use this to develop your own charts that are specific to you and your child. I have provided some suggestions; you know yourself and your child and will, I hope, be able to use my suggestions to find a solution that works for your family.

Introduction

The complexity and profound nature of the impact of early trauma led to a group of scientists including Bessel van der Kolk to make the case that a diagnosis of developmental trauma disorder should be included in the *Diagnostic and Statistical Manual of Mental Disorders, 5th edition* (DSM-5 is the standard classification of mental disorders used by mental health professionals). Van der Kolk believed that developmental trauma disorder provided the best diagnosis to date to explain the multifarious ways in which childhood trauma impacts children and the reason why trauma has such a long-lasting affect, even after children are removed from their traumatic surroundings and placed in loving families.

While neither the DSM-5 or the *International Statistical Classification of Diseases and Related Health Problems, 10th revision* (a medical classification list from the World Health Organization) include van der Kolk's definition in their latest editions, I believe that the term developmental trauma disorder does offer a useful description of the impact of early trauma that encompasses the breadth and depth of the difficulties experienced by traumatized children and their caregivers.

Van der Kolk stressed that early traumatic experiences:

- engender intense feelings of rage, betrayal, fear, resignation and shame – feelings that could be triggered by relatively minor stressors

- can cause traumatized children to re-enact their traumas behaviourally in subsequent environments
- can permeate relationships with caregivers, siblings, peers and teachers, often for many years to come.

According to van de Kolk (2005), all of these problems are expressed in dysfunctioning in multiple areas: educational, familial, peer-related, legal and work-related. Van der Kolk's work on the impact of early trauma has engendered a great deal of research into how traumatized children can be helped to cope with life. There are several books and articles aimed at helping caregivers provide an environment that is conducive to helping these children begin the repair processes that will help them manage lives in healthier ways. I've listed some useful further reading at the end of this book.

The book you're reading has evolved as part of this body of practice, the aim being to offer caregivers practical ways to parent their children using the principles of developmental reparenting espoused by Dan Hughes, Caroline Archer and me, among others. It is these authors' belief that developmental reparenting has been shown to be effective in helping children reduce their trauma re-enactment, develop self-esteem and promote healthy attachment relationships. They also believe that developmental reparenting promotes a less stressful, happier and healthier family life for every family member. These are the guiding beliefs that have informed the strategies and suggestions offered in this book.

While this book was primarily written by and for parents, I believe that the principles inherent within it have wider significance. Because families do not live in isolation, traumatized children are exposed to a range of environments in addition to family life. Without an understanding of developmental trauma disorder and developmental reparenting, a traumatized child's wider family and friend networks, peer relationships and school can add stress and reduce the child's ability to feel safe and secure. For optimal healing, children need a coherent and consistent approach across the range of environments that are part of their daily lives. I therefore recommend that the principles inherent in this book are shared with the friends, families and teachers who play a significant role in the child's life. I hope this book will then help towards a shared understanding of the impact of early trauma.

While some of the strategies are parenting-specific, many are transferable to other environments, including school. Indeed, it should be possible, with some creativity, to incorporate even the parenting-specific strategies into a child's wider environment; for example, sibling rivalry issues may be reflected in children who find it difficult to share with peers in school. An integrated approach permits parents and teachers to create the consistency and understanding that show children that adults can safely work together to help them. It also reflects the struggles traumatized children experience in managing changes in their environment, structure and routine. Seeing their parents and teachers 'singing from the same song sheet' will help children make sense of a world that often feels out of control, thereby reducing their fear-based responses.

The principles of developmental trauma disorder and developmental reparenting, and therefore the strategies and suggestions offered in this book, have relevance to children living in a variety of environments. While research into developmental trauma disorder and developmental reparenting rose within the adoption and fostering arena, early traumatic experiences are not the exclusive preserve of looked-after children. Children who are living in residential settings or in kinship care are likely to have been exposed to profound and life-changing traumatic experiences. Many children who have experienced domestic violence, neglect, abuse, parental disharmony, drug and alcohol abuse and parental mental health difficulties, including post-natal depression in their early months and years, live within their birth family. Babies who were born prematurely and spent time in hospital, or who had a range of medical conditions including severe colic, may have experienced the world as an unsafe and frightening place, despite parental efforts to relieve their distress. All of these experiences may have traumatized a developing baby, meaning that they are likely to benefit from developmental reparenting.

While developmental reparenting is an essential tool to help traumatized children begin the repair process, the principles and practices that are inherent within it provide a good starting point in parenting non-traumatized children. Indeed, the principles of developmental reparenting embody a way of relating and interacting that, if embraced, would be beneficial for all human relationships. This is a bold statement, perhaps, but one which has validity and worth.

Early trauma has a major impact on children's ability to form healthy attachments; i.e. the ability to recognize that they are entitled to feel safe, secure and loved and that they can rely on their caregivers to meet their needs. It also has a major impact on the executive functioning skills that make learning possible. Executive functioning is an umbrella term for the neurologically based skills involving mental control and self-regulation, i.e. a set of processes concerned with managing oneself and one's resources in order to achieve a goal.

The primary focus of this book is therefore to consider the ways in which early trauma impacts a child's ability to form healthy attachments and influences their capacity to develop the executive functioning skills that make learning possible. In essence, both attachment and executive functioning difficulties are a consequence of early trauma and of developmental trauma disorder. For this reason, both attachment and executive functioning difficulties must be understood with reference to a child's earliest traumatic experiences – as two fundamental outcomes of early trauma and the way experiences of abuse and neglect have impacted children.

You need to consider not only what happened to your children, but what it did to them. For example, if you are caring for a sibling group you may assume that they have had similar experiences. However, this may be far from the case. Take the example of a parent who struggled to meet the needs of one child, and who experienced even greater struggles when attempting to parent subsequent children. In this situation, contrary to commonly assumptions, the younger child in a family may be more traumatized than the older sibling.

Age, stage and gender can also play an important part. Gender-related issues can lead to one child being favoured over a sibling. This can have implications for both the 'favoured' and the 'non-favoured' child as well as the relationship between the siblings. Both are likely to struggle with new carers who try to treat their children with equal amounts of love and attention: the favoured child may feel rejected while the non-favoured child experiences increased attention to them as threatening. Sibling rivalry issues are likely to increase.

To develop a real understanding of their child's experiences, parents and carers may need to revisit, or obtain detailed information about, their children's lives prior to their current placement. Thinking about the messages children are likely to have internalized as a result of these experiences can be particularly painful for birth parents and kinship carers. For example, a parent who has moved on from an abusive partner may want to put the past behind them. They are likely to struggle to revisit painful experiences, especially if they also have to think about the impact on their much-loved child. The impact of early trauma can lead to grandparents experiencing conflicted loyalties in relation to their own children, and may encourage reflection on the reasons why their adult children have struggled to parent. Shame, guilt and recriminations can all be factors that impact the ability of family members and carers to revisit the past.

While natural, these feelings need to be overcome. If you are a birth parent, the fact that you are reading this book suggests that you want to make a difference to your child's life. Holding this core belief in your mind will help reduce negative feelings and anxieties and encourage recognition that thinking about your child's early experiences is a positive step towards repair for both you and your child.

Teachers may have particular difficulties in understanding the needs of traumatized pupils. A detailed background history may be neither possible nor appropriate, especially in secondary school where children have different teachers with different roles and responsibilities. Training and support to consider the possible outcomes of early trauma and how this might present in school is essential in helping teaching and ancillary staff understand and address pupil needs. Such training should be offered to all staff and be based on developmental reparenting principles, which will help staff recognize that traumatized children express their inner fears, not in words, but in behaviours that can be challenging and difficult to manage. Operating from the principle that access to a pupil's inner world can be gained by understanding their 'behavioural language' is a good starting point.

While each child is unique, there are often themes that predominate a traumatized child's way of understanding themselves and their world. These can include the following feelings:

- I find the world a scary, crazy place.
- I can't trust that adults will keep me or keep me safe.
- I'm not worthy of having my needs met.
- I need to be in control of everything/I can control nothing.
- I need to be really good to guard against having to move again.
- I hate myself and know that if 'they' really knew what I was like they would hate me as well.
- I know they are going to give me away so I might as well act 'bad' to have some control over this.
- If I'd been a boy/girl it might have been different.
- It's my fault that I was abused/neglected/abandoned.
- It's my sibling's fault that I was abused/neglected/abandoned.

Consider these messages in light of your knowledge of your child's history and as a starting point in using this book. For example, children who are 'bullying' other children may be acting from a fear-based belief that they need to be in control to feel safe. Recognizing this will help you to begin the process of embracing the developmental reparenting skills that best reflect your child's needs.

Understanding the 'why' will provide you with a springboard for considering how to intervene successfully. If certainty is not possible due to lack of information, your 'best guess' is a good starting point. Looking at a child's difficulties with empathy and an attempt at understanding the underlying messages, even if your 'best guess' is somewhat 'off the mark' is unlikely to do any harm. However, interpreting the behaviour as naughty or 'bad' has the potential for disrupting relationships and causing friction, both of which are more likely to create more misunderstanding and ultimately to increase rather than decrease a child's difficulties.

In order to avoid the awkwardness of 'he or she' and 'his or her', and to make this book as accessible as possible to parents, family members, teachers and other professionals involved in child care, I have used the male and female pronouns intermittently throughout this book, in a way that I hope is balanced.

Christine Gordon

PART 1

UNDERSTANDING THE BEHAVIOUR AND HOW TO HELP

The Impact of Early Trauma

All adopted, fostered and looked-after children have issues they have to manage within their lives. All have experienced the loss of their birth families, sometimes in settings that have made the separation particularly harrowing. Many have suffered severe abuse and/or neglect within their early lives. Many, too, have undergone multiple moves, and possibly placement disruptions. Contact arrangements may perpetuate feelings that the world is unsafe and scary.

Children in birth families or in kinship care may have experienced parental disharmony, parental separation, painful medical procedures and parental mental health issues. All of these issues, either singly or together, may have had a profoundly traumatizing impact, particularly if they occur pre-birth or in a child's earliest months and years.

The raw material of the brain is a nerve cell, called the neuron. Pre-birth neurons are created and migrate to form the various parts of the brain, differentiating or specializing as they do so to govern specific functions in the body in response to chemical signals. This process of development occurs sequentially from the 'bottom up', that is, from areas of the brain controlling the most primitive functions of the body (such as heart rate, breathing) to the most sophisticated functions (such as complex thought).

Post-birth, a baby's brain continues to develop at an amazing rate. The neurons developed during the foetal period begin to form connections called synapses. In this process of creating, strengthening and discarding connections among the neurons, synapses organize the brain by forming pathways that connect the parts of the brain. These pathways govern everything we do, from breathing and sleeping to thinking and feeling. At its peak, the cerebral cortex of a healthy toddler may create two million synapses per second and by the time children are two years old, their brains have approximately 100 trillion synapses, many more than they will ever need. Indeed, by three years of age, a baby's brain has reached almost 90 per cent of its adult size, the growth in each region of the brain being largely dependent on receiving stimulation, which spurs activity in that region. This stimulation provides the foundation for children's learning and for understanding the world in which they live and has major implications in terms of the impact of early trauma.

Just as positive experiences can help healthy brain development, children's experiences of maltreatment, neglect or other forms of toxic stress, such as domestic violence, can negatively affect brain development. This includes changes to the structure and chemical activity of the brain (for example, decreased size or connectivity in some parts of the brain) and in a child's emotional and behavioural functioning. For healthy brain development, babies need parents who respond to their cries and to their expressions of pleasure consistently and appropriately. This strengthens the neural pathways that babies need in order to relate to others, particularly those who allow them to get their needs met, both physically and emotionally. If children live in a chaotic or threatening world, one in which their caregivers respond with abuse or chronically provide no response at all, their brains may become hyperalert for danger, or they may not fully develop. The neural pathways that are developed and strengthened under negative conditions prepare children to cope in that negative environment, and their ability to respond to nurturing and kindness may be impaired.[1]

Furthermore, stress experienced by a woman during pregnancy may have an effect on her unborn child, most likely mediated by the

---

1   See Gordon, C. and Archer, A. (2012) *Reparenting the Child Who Hurts: A Guide to Healing Developmental Trauma and Attachments*. London: Jessica Kingsley Publishers.

transfer of stress hormones across the placenta. Research published in the May 2007 edition of *Clinical Endocrinology* shows that from 17 weeks of age the amount of stress hormone in the amniotic fluid surrounding the foetus is positively related to that in the mother's blood.[2] This has major implications for an unborn baby. In adults, stress hormones which are pumped into our blood when we become anxious are good in the short term because they help our bodies deal with a stressful situation. However, if these levels continue for a long time they can affect our health, possibly making us tired, depressed and more prone to illness. The impact is likely to be much more pervasive in a developing foetus whose primary job is to develop the neurons for healthy living. Trying to do this in a stressful environment is likely to impair neural growth as energy is diverted to managing stress.

The impact of this on future development has been well researched. A paper in a 2013 edition (7 April) of *Science Daily* highlights the long-term impact of foetal exposure to excessive stress hormones in the womb – research that demonstrates the link between foetal exposure to excessive stress hormones and adult mood disorders.

For developing infants, pre-birth exposure to stress can mean raised stress hormone levels post-birth, which in turn can lead to infants becoming tense, fractious, demanding, 'jumpy', hard to settle or overly sleepy, 'poor feeders' and unresponsive – patterns of behaviour that are likely to persist over time. These babies can present challenges to even the most secure and stable parent; a parent who is struggling with drug or alcohol issues, who is experiencing domestic violence, or who is struggling with post-natal depression can find the challenge overwhelming.

This has major implications for parents, carers and teachers. If a baby's neural production has been impacted by stress pre-birth and if their 'bottom-up' development has been impaired, the building blocks for the ability to learn and develop are being set on a foundation that is

---

2   Sarkar, P., Bergman, K., Fisk, N.M., O'Connor, T.G. and Glover, V. (2007) Ontogeny of foetal exposure to maternal cortisol using midtrimester amniotic fluid as a biomarker. *Clinical Endocrinology* 66(5), 636–640.

less than secure. Future stress is likely to have a more profound impact on this stressed baby than on one who had fewer pre-birth stressors. If, as is the case with many babies, they are exposed to further stress by living with parents who are struggling, their ability to develop the synaptic pathways for healthy development is likely to be impaired.

This in turn impacts a child's ability to make sense of, learn from, and adapt to individual circumstances appropriately. Living in a stressful environment with less than optimal coping mechanisms is likely to be terrifying, particularly in an environment where the major source of stress is also the major source of survival. Rather than learning how to thrive, these babies learn how to survive. They may have little experience of feeling loved, secure and stable and do not have the knowledge to adjust their thinking when placed with caregivers who are offering love and security. They are likely to be driven by the pre-conscious survival strategies they needed in their earliest months and to interpret love and affection as potentially life threatening. For this reason, caregivers and teachers may need to find ways to help the children in their care to 'go back to go forward'; i.e. they may need to adjust their parenting and teaching methods to better reflect the child's ability. This book is an attempt to make this adjustment easier.[3]

---

3   See Hughes, D., Baylin, J. and Siegel, D. (2012) *Brain-Based Parenting: The Neuroscience of Care-Giving for Healthy Attachment.* New York: WW Norton and Co.

How Neurobiological Development Affects Behaviour

The impact of adverse childhood experiences on neurobiological functioning demonstrates why early experiences can have such a profound and long-lasting effect on traumatized children. In essence, the brains and bodies of traumatized children are 'hard-wired' to the expectation of trauma, affecting the way they see themselves, other people and the world around them. This, in turn, is translated into their beliefs and behaviours: beliefs that are based on profound feelings of fear and rejection and a behavioural system they have developed to 'protect' themselves as best they can from the fear that threatens to overwhelm them.

These belief and behavioural systems, which are an expression of neurobiological 'imprinting', can only be altered by helping children 'reprogramme' their brains by providing them with experiences that allow them to forge new neural pathways. It is not possible for children to do this on their own. Their neurobiological connections were developed within relationships and it is only within the context of different relationship experiences that the development of new neural pathways becomes possible.

To make sense of this, let's consider how some traumatized children express their feelings and what might underlie their behaviours. Believing they were responsible for all that has gone on in their lives, some children work hard to be compliant, smiley and helpful. They may present as having succeeded in managing their problems; however, beneath their attempt to be 'good' lies a traumatized child struggling to fit in to avoid further hurt. Other children may try to cope with the belief that they are to blame for the abuse they experienced by outwardly blaming everyone else for all that has happened or is happening to them.

Since fear and feelings of loss of control are at the root of their difficulties, traumatized children may seek, subconsciously, to control their lives, leading to major issues at home and school, where they may demonstrate disruptive and defiant behaviours. Feeling a deep sense of shame and believing that what happened to them was somehow their own fault, they are so scared of further rejection that they try to pre-empt what they 'know' will happen by behaving in a manner that 'invites' the rejection they fear.

Some children alternate between the extremes of both, presenting at times a 'victim' persona, while at other times acting out in an aggressive and controlling way. This can be particularly hard for parents whose children present as compliant, 'good' children at school or in other environments, but then act out their distress in aggressive and controlling ways at home. Misunderstanding and blaming of parents, overtly or covertly, may ensue.

Developmental Trauma and Attachment Difficulties

A baby's vulnerability and dependence mean that they arrive in the world with a number of pre-programmed, automatic behavioural systems already in place. One crucial behavioural system is the attachment system.

This system helps babies to survive because it programmes them to seek comfort and support from their caregivers, particularly when they feel anxious, distressed, frightened or confused. These attachment behaviours are designed to bring the vulnerable baby into close proximity with an adult who can provide protection, comfort and care. Attachment behaviour includes distress and engagement signals; for example, crying, clinging, fretfulness, smiling and displays of vulnerability. These behaviours are designed either to bring the attachment figure towards the baby or to propel the baby to the attachment figure. Babies are therefore born prosocial – they have a universal human need to form close affectional bonds. The other basic requirement, if babies are to increase their chances of survival, is to make sense of not just the other, but also the self. Indeed, the very sense of self only becomes possible by interacting with others. The quality of the interaction with the attachment figure therefore impacts a developing baby's sense of self. If babies are not able to understand and impact the way in which their feelings and behaviour interact with and affect the behaviour and feelings of their primary caregiver, attachment difficulties are likely to ensue. For babies to make sense of themselves and others, they need parents to act in a relatively consistent way.

SECURE ATTACHMENTS

Secure attachments are formed when children are born to parents whose caregiving is broadly sensitive, loving, responsive, attuned, consistent, available and accepting. Parents who are interested in and alert to their infant's needs and states of mind provide an environment in which their child feels loved and understood. In this environment, children develop a cognitive representation (an internal working model) of the self as lovable and worthy of having their needs met. Babies born to attachment figures who show interest and concern will also mentally perceive others as potentially interested, available and responsive at times of need. It is out of such relationships that secure attachments develop.

It is also out of such relationships that babies begin to make sense of the world around them as a safe and predictable place in which to grow and develop. Thus, the nature of the relationship between the child and parent not only impacts the child's ability to make sense of themselves and their significant relationships, but also their ability to make sense of the world around them.

INSECURE ATTACHMENTS

Insecure attachments are likely to develop in babies who are born to parents who lack the ability to be sensitive, loving, responsive, attuned, consistent and available. Insecure attachments are also likely to develop where babies experience their primary caregiver as unavailable, neglectful or abusive. Insecure attachments promote more negative representations of self and others. Insecurely attached children do not see themselves as loveable and worthy of having their needs met. They do not see attachment figures as being available and responsive, and they do not experience the world as safe and predictable.

There is no absolute consistency in the way that insecure attachments are defined, with differing authors describing them in slightly different ways. I have chosen to use David Howe's[4] three basic patterns of insecure attachment, namely avoidant, ambivalent, and disorganized/controlling.

---

4   Howe, D. (2011) *Attachment Across the Lifecourse: A Brief Introduction.* Basingstoke: Palgrave Macmillan.

Avoidant attachments are often seen in children who are born to carers who feel anxious and irritated when their children make emotional demands. These carers tend to distance themselves when their baby shows signs of distress. Furthermore, rather than attempt to understand their children and their state of mind, carers impose their own views of how 'good' children should behave and see themselves – typically, as children who do not make emotional demands on parents.

Children who develop avoidant attachments adapt to 'rejecting' caregiving by downplaying and inhibiting their emotions and feelings of need. In effect, they deactivate their attachment behaviour as a way of increasing parental acceptance, or to manage the parent's lack of responsivity and availability. These children learn that they can gain most parental attention when they behave as the parent would prefer them to behave. Characteristic of avoidant children is therefore a tendency to be emotionally independent, self-sufficient, self-contained and compliant.

Ambivalent attachments are likely to develop when carers respond to their children in an inconsistent way. In the child's mind, there is no relationship between their behaviour and how the carers might respond. In attempts to increase parental responsivity, ambivalently attached children increase their displays of distress, including crying, fretting, whining, attention-seeking behaviour, fussing, fractiousness and being very demanding. In effect, they hyper-activate their attachment behaviour in an attempt to overcome the caregiver's insensitivity and to increase their parent's predictability.

They may also hyper-activate their attachment behaviour to show increased distress in an attempt to make sense of a world that seems inconsistent and unpredictable. In essence they are making a vain attempt to make sense of a world that they feel powerless to impact.

Disorganized/controlling attachments are associated with children whose carers are physically or sexually abusive, neglectful, abusers of alcohol or drugs, chronically depressed, disturbed by unresolved feelings of loss and trauma, the victims of domestic violence, or any combination of these. In other words, these are children who have experienced abuse and neglect – caregiving that is dangerous, unpredictable, frightening and inconsistent.

Abusive and neglectful parents present their children with a psychological dilemma. Fear normally activates attachment behaviour, which is designed to propel children into close proximity with their attachment figure where they might expect to experience feelings of safety, comfort and care. But if the attachment figure is the source of the fear, the child experiences simultaneous feelings of escape and approach, which cannot be resolved. Fear and attachment are out of balance and the child cannot organize an attachment strategy to increase feelings of care and protection. In this situation, children will also struggle to feel that the world is a safe and predictable place, or to feel that they have any sense of efficacy.

Children whose parents are both abusive and neglectful have particularly difficult caregiving environments in which to survive. Their world is one of unpredictable violence and random neglect. They experience parents as either out-of-control and aggressive, or helpless and needy. In these conditions, children avoid being cared for; for them, care implies danger and hurt. They seek to be in control rather than be controlled. These children have survived by trusting only themselves.

The result is that children, often from a very young age, become bossy, aggressive, violent, self-abusive, self-endangering, fearful, helpless, sad and extremely difficult to care for. These are the children who, typically, represent a significant proportion of the looked-after population.

Developmental Reparenting

Developmental reparenting is a concept associated with parenting practices that developed within the adoption and fostering communities from attachment theory and research. However, as I have already emphasized, the principles of developmental reparenting have much wider implications.

As well as providing a way for parents or parenting figures to understand the needs of traumatized children who are adopted, fostered or in residential care, it can help anyone who has responsibility for a child who has suffered early trauma. In essence, developmental reparenting aims to find ways to help children repair from the trauma of their early life experiences, and can be used by parents, parenting figures, teachers and indeed anyone with a significant relationship with the child.

School-aged children spend many hours in school and will benefit from an approach based on developmental reparenting principles. Grandparents and wider family members who embrace developmental reparenting principles can have an important role in supporting parents and parenting figures as well as helping the child to begin the journey towards healthier ways of interacting and understanding themselves and their world.

The primary focus of this book is to provide practical and manageable strategies to put developmental reparenting into practice within the range of environments that traumatized children experience.

The charts that feature in the second part of this book address a number of 'common' behavioural challenges; they outline some of the potential underlying reasons for these challenging behaviours and offer strategies and advice. The advice is based on the principles of developmental or therapeutic reparenting as explained previously and outlines the potential attachment and executive functioning issues that might underpin the behaviours. Suggested strategies for managing these behaviours are also given.

The charts are each spread over facing pages for ease of reference, but are also available to download as a single A4 sheet for anyone wanting a printable version to pin to a wall or fridge.

> The charts, along with supplemental resources for parents and carers, can be downloaded from www.jkp.com/voucher using the code GORDONPARENT.

As well as forming an effective basis for helping children begin the process of repair from early trauma, developmental reparenting can also help those who are involved with traumatized children to feel more in control of themselves and the child, with potential to encourage a happier and healthier life for everyone.

However, it is not easy to alter the 'traditional' methods and habits of interacting that we learned as children and which may now continue to be promoted by family, friends and the wider community who surround you. In the early stages of putting the principles of developmental reparenting into practice, some of the suggested strategies may seem to be counter-intuitive. This may make it even harder to embrace the principles.

As we have seen, when considering the most appropriate developmental reparenting approach for a traumatized child you need to think about all aspects of their functioning and how trauma affects them physically, emotionally and intellectually. You also need to consider how you were parented and the impact of your own past experiences; we all come to parenting and interacting with children with an attachment history that will impact the way we parent and interact with them.

Understanding your attachment history will help you to understand the 'buttons' and triggers you have and which traumatized children are likely to press. Doing this will also allow you to feel safe enough to explore your responses and make the changes that will provide a safe environment for the traumatized children in your care to do the same.

Remember, parenting is a very challenging task and we often berate ourselves when we make the inevitable mistakes. What can help is to recognize that we don't have to be perfect to help our children begin the repair process. We are all human and losing our temper and shouting at our children is inevitable at times. Apologizing and repairing the inevitable disruption in the relationship that anger engenders will repair the relationship and help children understand that they also don't have to be perfect to be 'good enough'.

MAIN PRINCIPLES AND CONCEPTS OF DEVELOPMENTAL REPARENTING

Developmental reparenting starts with a recognition that all aspects of a child's functioning can be impacted by early traumatic experiences. It also starts from a recognition that traumatized children have emotional 'gaps' they need help to fill in. In order to fill in these emotional gaps, children may need to 'go back to go forward'.

For example, children who have not had their dependency needs met might present as controlling and prematurely independent, insisting that they do not need help or assistance to wash, dress and so on. Progress for this child could be an increase in dependence: seeking help to tie shoelaces may be seen as progress, but is a different way of thinking to perceived wisdom that promotes the ability to tie shoelaces as an indication that children are progressing and developing.

Carers or teachers of a child who seems to be well behaved and compliant may perceive 'naughtiness' from this child to be out of character, or a sign that the child is struggling. Instead, naughtiness may be an indication that your child is starting to trust enough to let you see the 'real child' underneath the 'good' behaviour.

To integrate developmental reparenting into your daily interactions with a traumatized child you need to:

- start with an understanding of the child's history, remembering to consider not only what happened to the child, but what it did to him

37

- recognize how this affects the child now – body, brain, behaviour and cognitive
- recognize that children give us access to their inner world through their behaviour rather than their words
- recognize how early trauma impacts the child's understanding of the intentionality behind others' actions. Children who have been traumatized by abuse, neglect and abandonment may well interpret benign interactions in the light of past experiences and reinterpret kindness as abuse
- recognize the impact on you, including the impact of your own history. Children with challenging behaviours are likely to trigger negative feelings in the adults who are charged with their care. We all have an attachment history; often the behaviours that trigger our most negative feelings reflect our own attachment history as well as the challenges of managing the child's behaviour.

Moving from asking what this child is doing to asking what this child is trying to tell you allows you to change from being angry when children struggle to tell the truth, take things that do not belong to them, shout, swear or are angry and rejecting, for example, to wondering what they are trying to 'tell' you by their behaviour. Recognizing that fear underlies the child's difficult behaviours helps you interpret lying, for example, as a self-protective measure designed to ensure safety; stealing as a way of reducing feelings of abandonment; aggression and anger as fear responses to feelings of rejection.

While change and unpredictability are natural aspects of life, we need to recognize that abuse and trauma often occur in environments beset by chaos and uncertainty. You may, therefore, need to work hard to create an environment that is as predictable and consistent as possible, an environment where children are aware of the rules and expectations and where they are helped to manage these. When change is inevitable, recognizing the potential impact on children will help them manage this better.

For example, many traumatized children struggle when their teacher is absent and they have a supply teacher instead. Schools and parents can work together to prepare children for changes such as these. This, in turn, is likely to lessen the fear that changes of teacher could engender and will also supply a practical example of adults working together in the interests of the child.

Children need to learn that you understand why they are struggling but they also need to recognize that there are consequences for behaviour; together these provide the impetus for change. Recognizing that a child may struggle to manage a supply teacher because this triggers feelings of abandonment is the 'why'; helping the child with these feelings and ensuring they attend school is the 'what' you can do to help reduce the potential for school refusal. Helping the child who has run out of class to complete extra homework as a result of what they missed during classroom time is the 'how' you can help them recognize that there are consequences for behaviour.

Developmental reparenting needs to consider brain development. While it is very complex, the brain can be divided into three main levels: the brainstem level, the limbic or emotional level and the cortical or thinking brain.

The brainstem is responsible for alertness, arousal, breathing, blood pressure, digestion, heart rate and other autonomic functions; i.e. it controls what we *do*. It relays information between the peripheral nerves and the spinal nerves to the upper parts of the brain. The limbic level is responsible for our emotions, behaviour, motivation and long-term memory; i.e. it controls how we *feel*. It controls how we respond to situations. The cortex is the thinking part of the brain and controls executive functioning, including self-control, planning, reasoning and abstract thought; i.e. it controls how we *think*.

While not entirely linear, brain levels develop at different times and in different ways; the brainstem is the first to develop, with the limbic level next, followed by the cortical level. This is important when considering the impact of early trauma. As a baby's first task is survival they need first and foremost to develop their brainstems. They then need to make sense of their emotional world so that they can interact with it – hence the development of the limbic level. The cortical, thinking brain is the last to develop and is dependent on the development of the brainstem and limbic brain areas. Access to the thinking brain is also dependent on how the brainstem and limbic areas respond to any given situation. For example, if a child is angry, sad or afraid, their limbic areas will be heightened and their brainstems are likely to be in an aroused state. Access to their thinking brain will be vastly reduced. This is crucial. Often carers and teachers try to rationalize and reason with children at the cortical level when the fear-based nature of their behaviour indicates that they are operating at the brainstem or limbic level. Developmental reparenting means recognizing that rationalizing with children who are operating from their brainstem or limbic levels is bound to be ineffective.

Using the term 'practising' highlights to everyone that learning any new skill takes time; everyone makes mistakes when they are practising anything new. Developmental reparenting begins from accepting that loving parents are the best 'agents of change' to help traumatized children. Friends, neighbours, teachers and the wider family and community support network can help both parents and children by adopting a developmental reparenting approach that supports the parent–child relationship. Developmental reparenting begins from a belief that parents and children are doing the best they can, but provides the opportunity to 'do things differently'.

It is crucial that the 'team around the child' recognizes this and does not, inadvertently, undermine the parent–child relationship.

The main concepts of developmental reparenting can be summarrized as follows:

- Practising
- Shared responsibility
- Going backwards in order to move forwards
- Recognizing that children's behaviour is their 'language of trauma'
- Knowing when and how to intervene verbally to help the child work out what happened and what to do differently next time
- Being clear about intentions before acting
- Helping children recognize what is going on for them
- Encouraging parents, carers, teachers and other professionals to look after themselves.

Developmental Trauma and Executive Functioning Difficulties

Alongside the issues that are deep-rooted in their attachments and history, many children demonstrate delayed development of their executive functions. These functions, which are the skills that underlie learning, form the basis for the problem-solving skills of everyday living. For example, being able to tidy a bedroom, undertake homework tasks or even to dress yourself requires being able to start the task, remembering how to complete the task, having the ability to complete the task, organizing the materials needed to complete the task and recognizing when the task has been completed satisfactorily.

Although some aspects of executive skills relate to the limbic (middle layer), most are generally seen to be cortical (top-layer) skills. Executive skills are also impacted by stress within the brainstem and limbic systems of the brain, and this needs to be taken into consideration when trying to address a child's difficullies in this area. Children cannot deal with cognitively-based interventions when they are stressed and feeling angry, fearful or upset.

For this reason, we can only help children develop their executive skills when they are feeling relatively safe, calm and relaxed. So, you may need to focus on other aspects of your children's functioning as a precursor to working on their executive skills. However, working to help children feel calm and relaxed using the skills inherent in developmental reparenting, while not appearing to be executive skills-based, can actually help them improve their capacity for learning and therefore their executive skills – a 'two for one' offer that has real value.

There is considerable variance in the classification of executive functions, but it is generally agreed that they consist of the skills that allow individuals to manage life independently, taking into account their age and stage, and to behave in a way that fits the 'norms' of the society in which they are living. For example, children who are of primary age are expected to attend school and to interact positively with other children and teachers, learning and engaging in the work of the class.

I have chosen to use the classification of executive skills identified by the Behaviour Rating Inventory of Executive Function (BRIEF), a tool developed by Gerard Gioia, Peter Isquith, Steven Guy and Lauren Kenworthy for PARiConnect specifically to assess a child's executive skills as demonstrated in their behaviour. The BRIEF specifies eight areas of executive functioning:

- Behaviour inhibition
- The ability to shift from one task to another
- Emotional control
- Initiation skills
- Working memory
- The ability to plan and organize
- The ability to organize one's materials
- The ability to self-monitor.

Executive skills develop from birth through to late adolescence, and the BRIEF researchers agree that the frontal and pre-frontal cortex make up the neurological base for executive functions, although other cortical parts of the brain are involved. There are differences in the timing of the development of executive functioning skills:

- Behavioural inhibition begins to emerge between 5–12 months of age.
- Working memory (non-verbal) begins to emerge between 5–12 months of age.

- Self-regulation of affect/motivation/arousal begins around five months and becomes more evident when locomotion develops.
- Verbal memory is evident in the three- to five-year-old and is internalized by 9–12 years.
- Cognitive and behavioural flexibility, fluency and creativity, the skills necessary to consider appropriate problem-solving strategies begin from six years upwards.

For executive skills to develop to full capacity, children need the adults in their life to act as external regulators, providing boundaries, giving guidance, support and encouragement and acting as role models in new situations. Children who do not have supportive adults during their early months and years or whose attachment figures fluctuate between nurturing and abusive are highly unlikely to develop executive skills to a level expected for their chronological age.

Indeed, the nature of children's difficulties with executive skills may reflect the timing of their traumatic experiences. For this reason, it is vital to consider the child's behaviours and their executive functioning difficulties in light of their past experiences. For example, although an 'acting-out' child needs to be helped to recognize the inappropriate nature of their behaviour and the impact this has on others, this must be in the context of understanding the underlying reasons for these behaviours.

Empathy and an understanding that a child's behaviour is the only language they can use to demonstrate the hurt and despair they are feeling needs to be at the core of your management of a traumatized child. This means managing children's behavioural presentation calmly, recognizing that anger could engender frightening memories of a chaotic and angry early home life.

This is not always easy. Your own attachment history is likely to have an impact on the way you manage the children in your care and we can all have a 'bad hair day'. It takes time and practice to master the principles of developmental reparenting that underlie the ability to help children develop their executive skills. You need to learn to forgive yourselves for your mistakes if you are to forgive children their mistakes.

You also need to understand the shame-based nature of a traumatized child's view of the world. Being able to do this means recognizing the difference between shame and guilt, i.e. the difference between feeling that doing something inappropriate means that you are a mistake (shame) and that the behaviour was a mistake (guilt). Traumatized children often struggle to separate themselves from their behaviour, so they feel shame about themselves rather than guilt about, for example, taking something that doesn't belong to them. Helping children feel guilt starts in toddlerhood when they begin to learn, for example, that pulling the cat's tail will hurt the cat, or that taking a sibling's favourite toy will upset their sibling. In order for this to occur, the developing toddler needs to be in a relationship with a loving and caring parent figure who conveys the twin messages that, while certain behaviours are unacceptable, the child has worth and that the loving nature of the parent–child relationship is intact.

In this way, children learn that they are not the sum of their behaviours. Being able to separate themselves from their behaviour means that they can continue to feel 'good' about themselves as intrinsically worthwhile, while recognizing that they might need to change some aspects of how they behave and interact with others. Feelings of guilt develop as part of this process and this is essentially an inner recognition of the difference between 'right' and 'wrong'.

Traumatized toddlers who are parented by abusive or neglectful carers are likely to learn a very different message. Instead of learning that they are intrinsically worthwhile and loveable, abusive and inconsistent parents convey the message that the child is the sum of their behaviours. This can lead to children internalizing a feeling that they are intrinsically unworthy and unlovable, and that they are their behaviours.

When such children receive messages about behaviour they 'hear' this a message about their intrinsic 'badness'. This is difficult for parents, carers and teachers when they need to reprimand 'bad' behaviour in a child. Although there needs to be a consequence for actions, this should be applied in a non-shaming fashion, which is not an easy thing to do.

Adopting a manner of speaking to children that emphasizes that they are loveable can help greatly. Throughout this book, I suggest possible comments that you could use to help children recognize that you understand their struggles while at the same time giving the message that, with support, they can do things differently. This, too, takes time and practice.

A non-shaming way of talking to a child who has stolen something might include a message of understanding why the child struggles to know the difference between his and other people's belongings, followed by offering to help the child to return the item. You might also want to add an affirmation of your positive regards for the child: *'Do you know I still like/love you even when I need to help you understand the difference between your belongings and your sister's.'*

The Behaviour Rating of Executive Functioning (BRIEF)

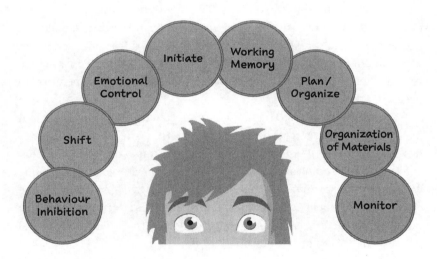

The BRIEF is a questionnaire that can be completed by parents, carers and teachers as well as by the child from the age of 5–18 years.

It asks a series of questions designed to elicit how well a child can decide what activities or tasks to pay attention to and which ones they chose to do. It assesses how well a child can manage novel or difficult tasks, including the ability to plan with a clear aim in mind, using anticipation, the selection of appropriate goals, not relying on habitual responses and using feedback constructively.

There are eight domains measured by the BRIEF and are the domains referred to in the tables which comprise the next part of this book.

BEHAVIOUR INHIBITION

This is the ability to stop your behaviour at the appropriate time, not acting on your immediate impulse. Children who have not developed their ability to inhibit are likely to react instantly to any form of provocation, albeit not necessarily intentional. The inability to inhibit one's behaviour can be a key factor in children diagnosed with attention deficit hyperactivity disorder (ADHD).

Creating a consistent approach to reduce fear-based responses will help a child with inhibit problems. This could be addressed by being clear about the house rules and expectations by, for example, making a poster that details the five most important house rules and placing it in a prominent place. Supporting your child in creating the poster will help to make her feel involved in the process and encourage co-operation in accepting the rules.

Parenting strategies to try include reinforcing appropriate behaviour by role-modelling and offering praise so that she knows what she has managed well. Remember to notice and praise the child for what she has stopped doing as well as what she has done; for example, playing with her brother for five minutes without arguing. Recognizing that some children do not feel good enough about themselves to accept praise, you must be specific in your praise – praise actions rather than giving global praise such as 'You are wonderful.'

You can help a child who has inhibit problems by working with her to recognize the triggers that impact her behaviour. Reminders before potentially difficult situations can help:

'I know you find it hard when I ask you to get ready for bed. So how about I give you a cuddle and we can talk through what you need to do to go to bed in a calm way?'

'I know it's hard to play with your brother. I can understand why you struggle when I think about how scared you were as a baby. I'm going to sit here for five minutes while you practise playing together.'

'I'm going to have to talk to you about something that I know you will struggle to hear. Can we do ten deep breaths together before our chat?'

Trying to create a calm home atmosphere can also help; for example, using music as a calming tool and reducing the number of toys. Children with inhibit problems manage better in a less stressful environment. Too many toys and a stimulating environment can raise general adrenaline levels and make it harder for them to feel calm and focused.

SHIFT

This is the ability to move from one activity to another and to make smooth transitions within any problem-solving activity. Children who experience difficulty with shift tend to be inflexible in their approach and can perseverate with an inappropriate response to a problem, for example struggling to understand why they have to stop playing to come for dinner despite repeated parental explanation.

You can help a child with shift problems by encouraging them to plan activities and think about the expected outcome. You might need to split the activities and outcomes into smaller steps and suggest they check with you after each part has been completed; for example, tidying a bedroom can be very difficult for some children. They might manage better by having a list of the component parts and checking with you when each part has been completed.

A five-minute warning might help, especially if this is accompanied by an empathetic: *'I know it's hard for you to stop playing when dinner is ready. I think you sometimes think that stopping playing now feels as if it's for ever.'*

A diary with the day's activities can help your child recognize that shift is an inevitable part of family life and allow him feel more comfortable with this. Discussing the plans for the day with reference to the diary might help, as will placing the diary in a prominent place as an aide memoire for your child. Getting him to participate in the planning of the day's events and writing or drawing the plan will give him a sense of ownership and involvement in family life. However, be prepared to do 'diary planning' by yourself if your child refuses to participate: *'Brilliant, I get to choose what we do today. Good for me!'*

Suggesting that the child practises a task for just five minutes or less might help reduce the repetitive nature of his difficulties, especially if you find ways to praise the positive aspects of what he has achieved as well as to think of what he might do differently next time; for example: *'Well done for putting your pants and socks on, let's see you manage with your trousers and top.'*

Try a 'praise sandwich': praise what he has achieved, then say what he might do even better next time (the filling), and then repeat the praise.

Role play situations that he is struggling with to show him a new way of managing that situation. Talk through what you are doing and why.

EMOTIONAL CONTROL

This is the ability to modulate emotional responses. Children who have not developed emotional control can become extremely angry, saddened, disappointed or overly joyous with little provocation.

They are subject to frequent mood changes. Emotional outbursts can resemble those of a toddler because their ability to control their emotions is still at the level of a toddler. Emotional control is not an executive skill that children can learn on their own; they need to learn this in a relationship with an adult who is calm and supportive. Emotional control is also a skill that takes practice and time.

Children who struggle with emotional control issues need, like a toddler, the calming presence of an adult to help them regulate their emotions. They may also need help to understand and connect their inner world (their feelings) to the outside environment (what is going on around them).

This is something that 'good enough' parents begin to help their children with from babyhood when they recognize the difference between their baby's hunger cries, their need for a nappy change or a call for attention, and they communicate this to their child. They add to this during toddlerhood by naming their child's feelings and the reasons for them: *'Goodness, I can see how angry/sad/happy you are. I guess you're feeling that way because I said no to that biscuit/when you have to say goodbye to your daddy/when we have a hug.'*

Naming your child's feelings and your best guess as to the underlying reason should be a regular part of your interaction with her as should naming your own feelings and the reasons for them. *'Today I feel happy because we're going to visit Gran.' 'I feel angry just now because I've burnt the toast.' 'I feel sad when I can see how hard it is for you to know that I love you.'*

Playing games about feelings can help. Make a face that demonstrates a feeling and ask her to guess the feeling. Encourage your child to make their own facial expression for you to guess.

Injecting a note of humour by getting it wrong might help to encourage conversation.

You could use one of the many 'feelings charts' that are available online; even better, create your own feelings chart with photographs of you and your child demonstrating varying feeling states. Use this to check with her how she and you are feeling at various points of the day.

INITIATE

This is the ability to start a task independently. It also involves independently generating ideas and problem-solving strategies. Children who have difficulty with initiate can sometimes be considered lazy or accused of not listening to instructions. However, children with initiate issues can struggle even when they are being asked to begin a task they enjoy. For example, a child might struggle to begin homework if asked to write a story about their favourite TV character, even if they enjoy talking about the programme and show interest in sharing this.

Dealing with a child who can complete a task with ease one day but not another is difficult; it might feel as if your child is being deliberately obtuse and difficult. This can make it hard to be empathetic and supportive. Reminding yourself that your child is doing the best he can will help you to remember that he may not be being deliberately stubborn or lazy. Instead, his initiate difficulties may be an indication of emotional control issues and feeling unsafe and insecure.

Current experiences often trigger past feelings of abuse and abandonment and these feelings will interrupt his ability to begin and master tasks. For this reason, noticing fluctuations in your child's ability to initiate tasks is a key to his inner world can help you find ways to enable him to feel safer and more secure. Reminders that he is now safe, alongside an acknowledgement that he might not feel like this, will help both you and your child.

A child who has initiate issues will need help to begin activities and to follow through tasks to completion. He might also need help during activities to remember the next stage. Gentle reminders about what the beginning, middle and end of a task look like might help. These reminders could be verbal or visual. For example, having a chart of your child undertaking the various steps needed to complete the teeth-brushing routine next to his toothbrush with a tick box might help. Making up a tooth-brushing song might also help if you sing it to your child as he engages in the task.

Many parents express disquiet about their child's 'addiction' to computer games. While limiting computer use may be important, using this interest might help your child with other tasks. The instructions involved in computer games are usually clear, precise and frequently repeated and there are many games that you can use to work through the tasks involved in everyday activities; for example, dressing-up games.

Limiting choices for children who have difficulty in making decisions will help. Choosing a treat from the plethora available may be too hard. Instead, you could help him practise by offering a choice between two treats and gradually increasing this when he seems to be managing.

However, please remember that, even after seeming to master making choices, your child may still find this overwhelming at times. Use these times as indicators that your child is struggling to feel safe, rather than an indication that he is being difficult.

WORKING MEMORY

This involves the ability to hold information in your mind in order to complete a task. Children who show difficulty in this area tend to forget complex instructions and cannot manage multi-step tasks. Seemingly simple tasks like teeth brushing involve a number of steps that can feel overwhelming to a child who struggles with working memory.

The strategies identified above for children with behaviour inhibition, shift and initiate difficulties will also help children with working memory issues. Visual and verbal reminders, mnemonics, rhymes and songs for everyday activities will help develop working memory. Talking through the ways in which you remember things might also help.

Use games to help develop your child's short-term memory. Card games that involve remembering hidden cards can help. You may need to start with picture cards and a limited number of them, and gradually increase the number of cards as your child's memory improves. That way you are helping your child build from success and you can offer praise when she gets it right.

Keeping the environment uncluttered in school might also help children who have working memory issues, as will having a clear plan for each task outlined clearly on the whiteboard. Consider whether your home and your child's bedroom is set up to help her with memory issues. Too many toys and distractions may not be in her best interests.

Talking about the plan for each day at breakfast and having this displayed in a prominent place can help your child develop memory skills, as can keeping reminders concise and simple. Offer one element of the task at a time and ask your child to repeat what she has been asked to do before beginning. Ask her to 'report back' at the end of each element of the task, at which point you can praise her and remind her of the next step.

PLAN/ORGANIZE

This involves the ability to manage present and future task demands. It relates to the ability to set a goal, plan the steps required to achieve the goal, and work through those steps in a timely and organized manner. Even something as seemingly simple as brushing your teeth requires a complex series of steps to achieve the goal of having clean teeth. To achieve this involves going into the bathroom, picking up your toothpaste, opening the toothpaste tube, picking up your toothbrush, putting toothpaste on your toothbrush, brushing all of your teeth, rinsing out your mouth, rinsing your toothbrush and putting it away and replacing the top of the toothpaste and putting it away: a minimum of 11 different procedures!

Supporting your child to plan and achieve can be undertaken using the strategies highlighted above, meaning that you have the potential to tackle two or more of your child's issues with one activity – a two-for-one or maybe a three-for-one offer that has real benefit for you and your child in helping him with other executive skills while addressing his ability to plan and organize.

Use of a Goal, Plan, Do and Review strategy will help – at home and in school. This could usefully be employed as classroom strategy to ensure that children understand tasks set and how to complete these. At home, if the goal is for your child to tidy his room, you can provide a picture of what a tidy room looks like and have this pinned to his bedroom door. Planning could include putting toys into their boxes, replacing books, a 'food hunt', looking for laundry, making the bed. Pictorial representations of all of these steps could be used to help your child.

Perhaps you could have each step on a separate card. You could encourage your child to complete each task in turn and return to you to report progress. This will allow you to see what your child has done, and you can praise efforts made and review the next step using the praise sandwich approach discussed above. You might want to turn the 'food hunt' or the laundry search into a game, with a prize for the person who finds the most socks. This needs to be done with humour to reduce the possibility that your child will see it as criticism.

Since your child might struggle with a task he has been able to undertake one day but not another, making a video recording of your child tidying his room when he is managing to be used when he seems to be struggling might be a good idea. Watching this together and reflecting on the tasks involved and how well he had tidied his room on the video will not only provide a run through of what is expected, but also convey a positive message that he *can* manage. If this is not a task your child can manage on any occasion, you could make a video of you tidying his room. In both instances, it is vital that you supplement the actions with words, perhaps using humour and exaggeration as you do so: *'Now I'm tidying the socks. Let's see? Five single socks. Eek! That sock alien must have transported their partners to the alternative sock universe. NO, phew! There is one on the bookcase and I think I can spot another one under the bed.'*

If your child is still struggling to plan and organize his life, try to show empathy and praise whatever he has achieved. Remember that you are helping him to practise the skills he will need for daily life and that such practising takes time and effort.

Songs and mantras might help your child keep to task especially if they end on a positive note.

Visual reminders can be of your child completing the tasks, or you completing the task. You could also use cartoon, film or book characters that appeal to your child; researching films or videos that show favoured characters doing household tasks could add some humour to the situation.

Modelling your own Goal, Plan, Do and Review strategies for your child's day-to-day tasks might help. If you are planning a shopping trip, you could talk through your goal of needing to shop for necessary food items, then talk through the procedures you need to undertake to complete the task; for example, finding your car keys, getting the shopping bags, making a list, deciding which shops you need to go to.

ORGANIZATION OF MATERIALS

This is the ability of your child to organize her resources, including her room, homework and school-bags. Difficulty with the organization of materials is often seen in the interplay between school and home, with children struggling to either bring homework home or return it to school. School equipment can also be lost in transit.

Children who experience difficulty in organizing their resources would benefit from concrete support for this.

- A credit card-sized visual reminder can help children remember which clothes to bring to and from school and can be attached to their school bag for easy reference.
- A colour-coded timetable that is replicated at home and school to match the reminder cards is useful.

- Laminating the cards adds extra life to them and saves them from tearing off but a non-laminated, regularly replaced system would allow for adding extra resources needed for that particular week's lessons. Given that setting up this system takes time, it may be time-saving to have another set available in case your child loses the first set.
- Working with the school so that your child has two sets of books, one for home and one for school, might help as an interim measure, as would arranging for an email exchange about homework required and tasks completed. Present this to your child as a loving gesture to help her manage, alongside a message that you have confidence that with some practice and by working together you can help her be more organized.
- Role play, model and talk through the methods you use to organize yourself and your belongings.

MONITOR

This involves the ability to monitor your behaviour, i.e. to see your behaviour as others perceive it so that you understand the effect it can have on others. It also includes being able to monitor your work and achievements in the light of the expected outcomes for the task.

Children who are unable to monitor their work tend to make mistakes and do not have the ability to recognize when they, for example, have not cleaned their room to a satisfactory standard. They may struggle to recognize the frustration felt by parents and teachers, who have to offer constant reminders.

Being able to monitor your behaviour is a complex task that involves a range of skills. It is an executive skill that depends on having a degree of emotional control and maturity. It is, therefore, a skill that needs to be built on the foundation of other executive skills. However, there are ways to help your child with this executive skill while he is working on his other skills.

Use of signals like thumbs up, down and sideways, or comparing views can help. There are also a number of charts and tools available to help children recognize their feelings and the difference between these and your feelings; for example, a 'feelings chart' comprises a range of faces showing a number of emotions. These charts, which are obtainable from the internet, can be used to help children express their feelings and explore similarities and differences. You could also research cards and games that explore a range of feelings.

Helping your child recognize not only what your expectations are but also your thinking process will help him to develop his thinking process. However, you need to take care to offer feedback in a supportive and non-shaming way.

It may be important to run through expectations in advance of asking your child to complete a task. For example, if one of your child's tasks is to load the dishwasher, you could remind him of this towards the end of the meal and talk through what a properly loaded dishwasher looks like.

A pictorial representation of this might help, as would a discussion about the order for loading the dishwasher and a request that he lets you know when he's loaded the cups so that you can remind him that the next task is to load the plates. This will allow you to offer praise for what he has achieved and encouragement to achieve the next component; and he may get so fed up with having to check in that he loads the dishwasher correctly first time!

Offering your child the opportunity to assess his success might also help, as long as you do this in a supportive way: *'I've noticed that you've stacked all the plates really well. Well done! I'm wondering what you think about the cutlery that's on the work surface. Do you think that also needs to be in the dishwasher?'* If your child says yes, you can then congratulate him on figuring it out. If he says no, you can be surprised that you and he think so differently about the same job, and then encourage him to do it your way.

If you have a partner you might want to talk about similarities and differences in perception about various aspects of daily life. For example, if you and your partner load the dishwasher in a different way, you could discuss why you do it your way while your partner asks relevant questions and offers her way of doing it and why.

Comments and Phrases that Support a Traumatized Child

In caring for traumatized children, you need to recognize that children's behaviour is the only 'language' they have to 'talk' to us about the sadness and fear that permeate their inner world. It's crucial that people caring for a traumatized child start from this standpoint and work hard to recognize that, while the child's behaviour may be directed at them, it is not really about the parent–child or teacher–child relationship. Instead, the bulk of the acting-out behaviours demonstrated by traumatized children reflect the abuse, neglect and abandonment they experienced when they were living within their birth homes and potentially within the care system, where they may have experienced multiple transitions including foster and residential care. Indeed, they may also have experienced multiple carers within birth homes – care arrangements that may have felt far from safe and nurturing and that are unlikely to be detailed in the child's life story information. In essence, traumatized children's behaviour is a manifestation of an inner world that is likely to be permeated by feelings of fear. It therefore provides a way in to understanding these children and the roots of their difficulties.

Often carers struggle with the fact that, at times, traumatized children seem to manage behaviour or situations that on other occasions they struggle with. It can seem that the child's behaviour is a deliberate attempt to thwart adult authority or that the child is lazy.

Understanding the child's trauma, attachment and executive functioning difficulties allows you to recognize that rather than 'won't do', children 'can't do'. You will never know all the triggers to children's early experiences. These experiences can catapult them into the defensive behaviours they 'learned' in their early months and years and which interfere with their capacity to manage their environment in the here and now. Recognizing the impact of this on a child's attachments and executive functions will help you create the optimum environment for your child to succeed rather than fail. It also allows you to demonstrate empathy and understanding towards your child.

Talking empathically to children has two advantages. It helps them to know you understand their difficulties in managing their behaviour and it can help them understand their own difficulties, thus improving self-monitoring skills.

Children who started life without a 'good enough' parental model to validate their thoughts and feelings need extra help to understand that the world can be benign and that adults can be trusted. The fear that lies at the heart of a traumatized child's behaviour and the traumatic nature of their experiences are likely to dominate their understanding of the world, their relationships and their place within these. Offering empathy for your child's struggles helps to redress the balance and lets him know you are there to help rather than to criticize and blame.

Supportive and understanding comments might include:

'I understand you're having a problem with this. I'll help you to practise... Don't worry if you struggle. Practising means it's okay to make mistakes.'

'I can see you're not managing today. Let's...'

'I know you'll have difficulty managing this so instead we'll...'

'I thought this would be hard for you. Don't worry, we can try it another time when you've managed to practise a bit more. Instead, I thought we could...'

'I know you have more trouble with this than most of your friends and I understand why that is. I can help you practise the things you struggle with.'

'Thank you for showing me you can't manage this today. It lets me know I'm getting to know you well.'

'Hurting your sister has shown me you are finding it very difficult to manage your emotions today. I think we need to… I also need to give your sister a cuddle so that she knows she's special as well.'

'I know you find this very hard. You have two choices; either you…or you can… Do you need help in choosing?'

'I can see this was too difficult for you today. That's not a problem. We can try something you will manage today and I can help you with…on a day when you might manage it better.'

'You didn't have a mum to help you manage your feelings when you were a baby. That's why it's so hard for you now and why you need me to help you. I'm so glad I can help you with this.'

Praise and Reprimands, Consequences and Rewards

PRAISE

Sadly, some children spend the first months or years of their lives being told how bad they are. For others, their lack of worth may not be expressed in words but in actions or lack of action. Being beaten, punched, kicked, bitten or burnt is more than enough to demonstrate to anybody that they are unworthy of love or care. Parental disharmony and domestic violence can be a terrifying environment for any child. Having to find one's own food, being abandoned or living in squalor and excrement understandably will affect one's view of life.

Being placed for adoption as a baby can lead to profound feelings of worthlessness; feeling that you're not 'good enough' to be kept by the mother that gave birth to you can lead to profound feelings of rejection and lack of self-worth.

Pre-birth experiences can be significant. The impact of exposure to drugs or alcohol can be profound, even in babies who are not born drug dependent or who do not have a diagnosis of fetal alcohol effect. If your first months are spent battling for survival, you are likely to feel unloved, uncared for and unworthy of the right to life. For the developing fetus this can, in a very real sense, feel like rejection – a feeling that drugs or alcohol take priority.

When this is put into context, we can begin to see the dark cloud of shame under which traumatized children live. We may know that adults were responsible for the child's experiences; however, these children are likely to feel that they bear the bulk of the responsibility.

You may surmise that praising children will help to make them feel more positive about themselves; however, they may view praise as a threat to their sense of self. Feeling worthless can lead to feelings that your praise is unjustified, misplaced, a lie or a trick. Furthermore, praise for children who have been sexually abused may be linked with harrowing memories; the child might have been groomed with tales of how special they are. The fact that the child finds it very hard to accept praise or to be reprimanded is, therefore, easily understood. They desperately need praise to build up their self-esteem, especially when their inappropriate behaviours lead to the necessity for reprimands, yet this needs to be done in a way a child can tolerate and manage. 'Global' praise such as, 'What a good kid you are', or 'You're amazing' is often too much for a child who lacks any sense of self-worth. Instead, praise may be best offered for specific behaviour and activities; for example:

'I noticed how well you got dressed this morning. Well done.'

'Well done for not hitting your brother when he took your toy.'

'I've noticed how well you stood in line today. Well done.'

Statements such as these offer recognition and validation of the child and this in turn has the potential to lead to a healthier sense of the self as having worth and as therefore being loveable.

In summary, traumatized children desperately need praise to build up their low self-esteem, but they often find it incredibly hard to accept and believe praise. They may have a long-established belief in their lack of worth and cannot accept the praise that is given to them. Before you offer praise, you might want to let your chid know that you understand how difficult this is for them: *'I know you struggle to feel good about yourself, so you might find it hard to hear me say...'*

REPRIMANDS

Reprimands might be just as difficult for these children to hear. Your aim may be to let them know that you are not happy with a certain behaviour, but they are likely to hear it as a confirmation that they are worthless.

For this reason, try to help them succeed by suggesting tasks and making requests that are within their capabilities and be prepared to recognize that there may be occasions when tasks that are sometimes within their capability are beyond their reach at that moment. Please remember that they may be operating at a much younger age than their chronological age implies – think toddler.

Use comments such as: *'I can see that it's really hard for you to tidy your room today. I wonder if you're letting me know you don't feel good about yourself. Maybe if I give you a hug you will begin to feel good enough to get that job done so that we can go out and have some fun.'*

If you know they might struggle you should acknowledge this in advance. *'I think you may find it difficult to... Let's think about ways I can help you with this'* is an especially helpful phrase since it not only conveys a message that you have confidence that they can do things differently, but it also shares responsibility for the 'problem', giving a message that they do not have to manage alone.

Other helpful sentences include:

'I understand you find it very difficult to walk away when somebody is annoying you. Let's see if we can work out a way to help you do this.'

'I'm really sad you didn't manage to control your anger. I can show you ways you can be angry in a safe way. Why don't you try...'

'I know it's hard for you to know I love you when we have to talk about some things you've been struggling with. Can we figure out ways I can make it easier for you to remember that I love you and that I know you sometimes struggle with...?'

If you have to reprimand your child, keeping the reprimand succinct and focused enables them to recognize your awareness of the misdemeanour and their need to take responsibility for their actions while minimizing the possibility that shame will lead to anger, denial or dissociation. Don't expect them to tell you why they have behaved the way they have; they are unlikely to be able to answer you. Try to avoid long, drawn-out enquiries to elicit the truth. Don't be tempted to demand eye contact. A child does not need to look at you to hear you.

Children may be sinking in shame and imagining and predicting consequences in their mind before you even start talking. They are likely to know that you are going to reprimand them and are probably feeling ashamed and afraid of the potential consequences. It can be hard to remember this when faced with defiance and denial. Try to remember that a defiant front can be a desperate attempt by a child to hide the fear they are feeling. Their levels of stress-related hormones such as cortisol and adrenaline may be incredibly high, and their defiance may reflect this.

Alternatively, they may seem to be unaffected because they have 'dissociated', i.e switched off as a survival strategy.

Furthermore, children often have limited ability to process words, especially when they are feeling threatened. Their adrenaline levels are likely to be raised to a point that thinking and processing are reduced. They, literally, may not be able to hear what you are trying to say and are therefore unable to respond.

While these stances can be incredibly annoying and can lead to frustration, try to remain calm and focused. This is more likely to help them see that their behaviour does not automatically lead to rejection or abuse as it did in the past; this reduces fear, cortisol and adrenaline.

Children need to know that it is their actions you find unacceptable, not themselves. It is therefore vital that, as soon as possible following your reprimand, you let them know that they are worthwhile and can, with support, do things differently.

CONSEQUENCES

Having an understanding and empathetic approach is a necessary part of parenting and teaching, but children also need to recognize that there are consequences for behaviour. Without this, children will not feel that change is possible, meaning that they will be left with the feeling that the fear that threatens to overwhelm them is a 'life sentence' to endure. It also means they will be stuck in patterns of behaviour that, as they grow and develop, have potentially negative consequences that could impact all future relationships. If children are not helped to find ways to express anger in verbal rather than physical ways, the consequences can be profound; as adults, they could be prone to being perpetrators of domestic violence. If a dissociative child is not helped to recognize and express feelings there is a danger that, as an adult, they could become a victim.

Sanctions and consequences need to be specifically related to the behaviour and to be short term. These children are likely to struggle with a 'three strikes and you're out' approach, or consequences that build up in severity. Sanctions that build up in severity may encourage children to believe they are unable to manage and this could lead to escalating behaviour to 'get the consequence out of the way'. In effect, these children will live up to their own – and their perception of your – expectations to try to alleviate the suspense and to save themselves extra worry.

Waiting for a consequence will prevent a child from focusing on anything else. Try to ensure that consequences fit the behaviour, are short and completed sooner rather than later, and that the episode is then finished: a line is drawn under it, it is not counted towards further sanctions and not referred to again when the child does not manage next time.

There may be occasions when you need to think about how best to deal with a child's behaviour. There may also be occasions when anger predominates your thinking. Here I suggest you tell your child that you are struggling to think about how you can best help him, that you love him, need some time to get it right and that you will let him know what will happen when you've figured it out. If applied sparingly, this approach will allow you time to think and, perhaps, to seek advice from your family and friendship network.

Isolation can be traumatizing for children who spent much of their early life alone and neglected. Time out and the 'naughty step' are not appropriate sanctions for children who have experienced abandonment. Instead, where possible, you should keep your child close to you.

REWARDS

Rewards, too, should fit the behaviour and need to take place soon so that the connection is made between the behaviour and the reward. A reward will probably need to be kept low key, especially if children find it difficult to accept it as inwardly they feel unworthy of being rewarded. Indeed, they may wonder about possible underlying negative consequences of accepting a reward; this may be particularly true of children who have been subject to sexual abuse.

Talking about the reward in advance rather than offering it as a surprise may be a wise move as it reduces the suspense of 'not knowing'; children who have been abused often confuse surprises with further potential abuse. Offering a couple of choices might give children the opportunity to decide on a reward that feels most comfortable for them; however, you may need to help them make the appropriate choice until they feel sufficiently confident to voice their opinion.

Star charts are often ineffective with traumatized children, just as a star chart would not work with a toddler demonstrating tantrums. Working towards rewards can be setting these children up to fail and can lead to increased acting out. This may be because the child lacks emotional control and monitor skills. It can equally relate to lack of self-worth. Children who do not feel that they deserve rewards are not going to work towards them. Their lack of self-worth might also mean that they 'know' they will fail; this 'knowledge' may well lead to them giving up to ensure the failure that they know was inevitable.

SUMMARY

Frequent short breaks, limiting distractions, clear expectations and consistent rules, peer modelling, reinforcement of appropriate behaviour, limiting settings that are likely to provoke problems, adjusting requests to suit children's emotional maturity, helping them to develop an emotional vocabulary so they can verbalize their feelings and helping them to identify stress-inducing situations are all steps you can put in place.

Although traumatized children need structure, containment and consistent rules and routines, they also need an empathic, understanding approach. Verbally acknowledging the things they struggle with can validate their feelings. Many traumatized children have experienced a combination of loss, trauma, abuse, neglect and constant moves. They have had nobody to model self-regulation and some of the adults in their lives have caused them severe hardship. They may remain hyper-vigilant and guarded, unable to trust adults and feeling that they will only survive if they remain in control of their lives. They need to learn that they can begin to relinquish control and accept adult authority, but they will not do this in an environment that lacks structure and where they feel misunderstood.

Using phrases such as, *'I guess I would struggle with...if I had had a difficult start in life'* or *'I guess you are feeling very anxious at the moment'* can help.

Siblings

Many children in foster care or who are adopted are part of a sibling group and there is certainly a drive to place siblings together where possible. This drive emanates, in part, from the longevity of sibling groups; our sibling relationships are among the longest we are likely to experience, longer indeed than our relationship with parents and other important family relationships. This drive also emanates from a belief that siblings share a similar history and that placing siblings together is a protective factor in terms of placement stability.

While these factors are important when making decisions on sibling placements, this is only part of the story. Siblings may have some of the same background experiences; however, age and stage will determine how each child is impacted by these background factors. Neglect and abuse will be experienced very differently to a two-year-old as opposed to a baby or a five-year-old.

Furthermore, just because two (or more) children have been born into the same family does not mean that their experiences are the same. A parent who was struggling to offer 'good enough' care to one child may struggle more when faced with the prospect of parenting two or more children. It is not, therefore, a given that the youngest child in a sibling group will have experienced less trauma than the oldest child at the time they come into care. Indeed, the youngest child may have experienced significantly greater trauma during their early months than their siblings.

Gender differences may also play a part, as will the fact that one sibling might have experienced being the favoured child. This makes it difficult not only for the less favoured child, but also for the favoured child when the siblings are placed together with parents who are working hard to meet the needs of all of their children.

As always, the impact of early trauma is profound, impacting not only each child in a family but also the sibling group and the nature of sibling relationships. Each child will have developed a survival strategy and their own unique way of making sense of their experiences. Instead of placing responsibility for their traumatic experiences on the parents and carers who should have met their needs, they may have developed a belief that either they or their sibling was responsible for their traumatic experiences.

Siblings may also have developed different survival strategies with one child acting out in aggressive and angry outbursts, while another child may have become the 'good' child, working hard to comply with parental requests in the hope that this will reduce the possibility of further abandonment, neglect or abuse. Sometimes a compliant child will internalize their feelings but act these out in self-harming and other concerning behaviour. Sometimes siblings alternate between the two ends of the spectrum. Whatever the situation, both your acting-out and acting-in children need help and understanding to address the feelings that underlie their behaviours.

Children Who Act Out in Aggressive and Angry Behaviour

Aggressive behaviour may come in many guises and can include both verbal and physical aggression as well as comments that belittle another or incite feelings of helplessness and hopelessness. Children who are aggressive may demonstrate this in some relationships or in all relationships. They may be aggressive towards siblings and parents while demonstrating a submissive, victim role in peer relationships; they may flip between aggression and being submissive.

It might be tempting to view sibling aggression within a home environment as being 'normal' sibling rivalry and therefore minimize its impact on both siblings. It may also be tempting to minimize behaviour directed towards a parent figure, especially if the child is young; parents can view toddler aggression as relatively normal displays of anger, as toddler tantrums.

Neither of these stances is helpful for anyone. Aggressive behaviour is damaging to everyone in the family. It allows aggressive children to continue patterns of behaviour that are unhelpful and unhealthy, preventing them from exploring new and healthier ways to express their feelings and relate to others.

For the victim, the damage is more obvious; it is likely to create fear and resentment and reduce the victim's feeling of self-worth. It also reduces feelings of safety within a family. Aggressive behaviour is therefore something that should be addressed for the safety of every family member.

As always, you need to address the behaviour by looking with empathy and understanding at the possible reasons for the aggressive child's behaviour within the context of their past. For example, did the child's early experiences, including those pre-birth, involve physical abuse or witnessing domestic violence? Remember that children can 'witness' domestic violence even when they are in another room. They may well have lain in bed at night listening to parents arguing, shouting and crying while they worried about their safety and the safety of the parents on whom they depended for their survival. In this environment, children may have internalized a belief that aggression was the best form of defence against terror. Furthermore, their role model for expressing anger is likely to have come from a situation in which aggression played a significant part.

The child may have learned to disassociate from their angry feelings when living in this frightening environment and is only able to act them out when they are removed from the source of their terror; i.e. when they move into a home with parents who work hard to create a calm, loving and secure environment. Not having learned how to manage feelings of anger in an appropriate way, children may act these out in extreme ways. You need to show empathy for their history and the lessons they learned; remember that they did the best they could to keep themselves safe within an environment that was unsafe and frightening. You need to communicate this effectively to them.

Alongside this you need to consider the possible triggers for the behaviour in the present. Are they struggling to manage a perceived threat in the current situation? The perceived threat may appear to be a minor one until you recognize its resonance with their history.

Losing a game might seem overwhelming because it signifies a loss of control or a feeling of worthlessness – feelings the child may try to protect against by hitting out or by deflecting their feelings onto others. They may well be trying to signal their feelings in an unconscious effort to receive help. The same may be true when children are struggling with not being allowed to go first in a game or in any situation where they perceive, however unjustified it may seem, that they have lost control. You might want to role-model an appropriate response by becoming angry about losing a game and then demonstrating how to manage the feeling: *'I so hate losing and I feel really angry just now. I think I'll do ten star jumps and shout about how I feel to get rid of my feelings.'* After completion you could say: *'Phew! I still don't like losing but I feel much calmer now.'*

While it is true that rivalry permeates all sibling relationships, the extent of this is likely to be increased if children were raised in abusive and neglectful environments. A dearth of essential resources or positive parental attention may have meant that attention or food given to one child resulted in there being less for other children in the family. One child may have been favoured over other children in the family, leading to difficulties for both the favoured and the non-favoured child if they subsequently move to a home where parents treat all children in more egalitarian ways. Each child is likely to hold deep-seated but largely unconscious beliefs and feelings that attention given to a sibling has potentially disastrous consequences.

For such children, aggressive behaviour may be viewed as a survival strategy, as an attempt to ensure they are keeping themselves as safe as possible in an environment that feels inherently dangerous.

Disagreements with siblings and the consequent negative reaction of parents are likely to leave aggressive children feeling a sense of abandonment and aloneness. They are unlikely to have internalized a belief that they can turn to adults for help with their feelings, instead feeling that they must manage their emotions by themselves.

Neurobiologically, the child's body may be geared to produce high levels of stress-related hormones such as adrenaline and cortisol. Highly charged incidents allow the child to release some of this. This again may reflect the child's history and their survival strategy. The hormones that are produced when we are living in a stressful environment are difficult for the body to cope with; aggression discharges the hormones, offering the body some relief.

Remember that fear is at the heart of the behaviour; if you can reduce your child's fear, you are likely to reduce their aggression. You are also likely to reduce the level of stress hormones, thus reducing the need for them to discharge these hormones in angry outbursts.

Safety is a crucial issue for anyone caring for traumatized children. Instances of aggression may be displayed during unstructured and less-organized moments, possibly because children feel less safe in these environments. They are likely to have a reduced capacity to regulate their emotions meaning that, like a toddler, they need the presence of a supportive and calm adult to manage their behaviour and feelings.

Children can be wary of aggressive siblings and this can aggravate the situation; some may act out the role of 'victim' and seek out their sibling even if this leads to being hurt. For some children, this may be repeating patterns of interaction learned within their family of origin – the familiar is often easier to manage than the unfamiliar. Other siblings may therefore need help with their role within the sibling relationship; it is not healthy to act out or practise being either abuser or victim.

Aggression within a school setting can be particularly difficult to manage. Teachers have a duty to keep all children safe and need to be conscious of bullying; they must offer clear messages that aggression and bullying are not an appropriate response within a school or indeed any environment. This may not sit easily with the need to understand the reasons for the aggressive child's behaviour and the ability to demonstrate empathy and understanding.

Other pupils are likely to be fearful of an aggressive child and this can impact peer relationships, leaving the aggressive child feeling isolated and alone and increasing feelings of lack of worth, all emotions that are likely to increase the potential for acting out in aggressive outbursts. These issues are likely to be more difficult to manage in unstructured time; for example, in the playground where supervision is harder to maintain.

Having a school policy of 'zero tolerance' for aggression that is shared with all pupils might help, as will close supervision during unsupervized time. It might also be necessary to restrict an aggressive child's playtime activities to occasions when supervision is possible. This needs to be expressed to the child, not as punishment, but as an attempt at helping them: *'I know it's hard for you when you're out in the playground. I can understand why. You've not yet learned how to be angry in a safe way. Your parents and I are going to help you with this. Meanwhile, you need to be kept safe and the other children in the school need to be kept safe. For now, I would really like some help in sorting out the classroom. I know you're great at that.'*

It's not a good idea to allow aggressive children out into the playground in the hope that they will be able to manage, and then having to intervene when a fight breaks out. Instead, keep the child close and allow them the final five (or so) minutes in the playground to 'practise' being with other children in a non-aggressive way. This allows for greater possibilities of success and you can congratulate the child on beginning to play in a calm way. Children learn from success, not failure.

Compliant Children Who Internalize Their Feelings

It can be hard for parents and teachers to remember that the quiet and compliant child may have as many needs as the angry child and it can seem even harder to carve out time for this child. The angry, 'in-your-face' child may take up so much time and attention simply to manage the safety issues involved that there is little time for anything else. While the stresses involved in managing an out of control child are clear, it's important that the quiet child's needs are also prioritized.

As always, you need to begin by thinking about the child's history – the 'dictionary' that allows you to understand not only what happened to them, but what it did to them. Many factors may have affected their development in the womb, at birth and within the first months and years of life.

You need as much detailed information as possible to understand how the child is in the present. A compliant child may have developed a belief that they can minimize their exposure to abuse by doing as parents ask, no matter how unreasonable. They may have received messages that their needs were not important and that their role in life was to meet the needs of adults. They may have been so overwhelmed with fear that they found a way to switch off from feelings by dissociation.

Many traumatized children live in a heightened state of anxiety, partly because of their early life history of rejection, abuse or neglect. Indeed, recent research has shown that some children are born with a high level of cortisol as a default due to adverse experiences in the womb. Many of these children live under a shadow of shame. They feel they were not worthy of nurturing care and consider that it was their fault that they were abused. They were not 'good enough' to be loved. These children live in a world where they cannot believe that anybody truly cares about them.

Some of these children can disguise these emotions and show incredible aptitude at 'managing' how they inwardly feel. These are the compliant, people-pleasing children. They may act with responsibility and maturity; they may be helpful and keen to offer their time for others.

There are some children who can manage this within the school environment, when out with friends and on school trips but cannot continue their efforts at home. They may react negatively especially towards their adoptive mother, with school staff sometimes witnessing atrocious behaviour when arriving at or leaving school. The adoptive parents may describe behaviour at home that seems out of character for the teacher's knowledge of the pupil at school. Sometimes, it seems that something is 'wrong' at home and it can be easy for criticism to be aimed at the parents. Some children, however, can maintain this well-behaved demeanour in all aspects of their lives. It appears that they have come to terms with any issues regarding their early lives or adoption. They seem well adjusted, sensible, hard working and mature.

Compliant children may be working hard to maintain this behaviour. While they desperately want to be accepted by the adults in their lives and by their peers, they may well be living with a fear of rejection, feeling responsible for any rebuff they experienced in their early lives. If they have a brother or sister who is causing difficulties either at home or in school, they may feel they must behave well to compensate for their sibling's behaviour. At home, they may feel they need to be 'good' as their parents are experiencing enough problems with the acting-out sibling. There is a possibility that they have experienced the breakdown of the placement of a sibling, and fear that this could be replicated in their own lives.

Although compliant, people-pleasing children may do well, at school or home or both, there may come a point in their lives when they will have to confront the fact that this behaviour has been an 'act'. This point may not come until late adolescence or early adulthood, or even much later in life. It can be a traumatic time.

Compliant children who display a 'false' sense of maturity need to understand that less positive behaviours do not lead to rejection. They need to recognize that they do not need to meet the needs of adults to be acceptable; they need to be able to 'practise' knowing that they are acceptable and worthy of love even when they are being 'naughty', i.e. they need help to recognize that they are different from their behaviour and that unacceptable or inappropriate behaviour does not herald abuse and rejection.

Parents and teachers can achieve this by the example they set in their daily life. For example, talking about making mistakes and 'forgiving' yourself for the mistake. Understanding that the child's behaviour is their language, and demonstrating to the acting-out child that they have choices and that you will support them in making appropriate choices will demonstrate to the compliant child that rejection does not necessarily follow bad behaviour.

Since it is vitally important that the compliant child knows that they do not have to be 'good' all the time you may want to help them to practise being 'naughty' by, for example, tearing up newspapers together and throwing them about the room or by engaging in messy play.

If the child displays difficult behaviour the natural tendency is to reprimand the child or remark that this is out of character; it may feel like a backward step. However, going against perceived wisdom, 'naughty' behaviour from a compliant child might be a sign of progress, a sign that they are beginning to trust enough to show parts of themselves that were previously hidden.

If this is the case, then remarking on this might be appropriate: '*I noticed that took your sister's toy. I wonder if you're checking whether I can still love you when you're naughty. Why don't I give you a hug so that you know I love you; then we can return the toy together.*'

Pee and Poo or Choosing Your Battles!

This book suggests ways to manage a range of behavioural issues that traumatized children 'use' to express their trauma-based inner beliefs about themselves and the world in which they live. It emphasizes that traumatized children's behaviour is the only 'language' they have to express the fear that underlies their beliefs. While their behaviour is challenging for parents and can cause distress and frustration, it's important to recognize that children often 'can't do' rather than 'won't do'. This is as true of soiling and wetting as it is of the behaviour problems outlined in the charts. However, 'pee and poo' issues are not included in the chart, nor are there suggestions for managing these issues. This is because these are not behaviours that parents can effectively manage by using strategies and suggestions offered for some of the other behaviours that traumatized children display. It is extremely difficult for parents and teachers to successfully intervene in and manage elimination problems; instead, you may need to consider these issues in terms of the wider picture.

As always, this must start with a consideration of the why children might have difficulties in this area. It's important to think about the child's history – the 'dictionary' by which all behaviour can be understood. This means beginning by considering the child's earliest experiences.

Was your child left feeling uncomfortable and perhaps in pain in a wet and dirty nappy for long periods of time? This child would need to have found ways to manage the feelings this engendered. If so, this may have included dissociating from the feelings, a way of managing that may be continuing in the present; the child may soil because he does not recognize the signs that he needs to go to the toilet. He may, literally, not be aware of, or feel uncomfortable, when he has soiled. He may not have learned control over his bladder.

Control may also be an issue here. Indeed, control issues are often at the heart of many of the difficulties displayed by traumatized children. Thinking about the child's experiences will help to make sense of this. This child had no control over his early traumatic history. He had no control over being abused and neglected; he had no control over being accommodated or for moves within the care system; and he had no control over the decision to be placed with his current family. He may have internalized a belief that this this lack of control led to the traumas he suffered. Soiling and wetting is something that he may feel he has control over. Your frustration may, therefore, make it harder for the child to 'give up' soiling behaviour because it seems as if he is also giving up the only control he feels he has, with the potential that catastrophe may ensue.

Soiling may feel like a safety issue, particularly for children who were subject to sexual abuse. Pee and poo may have kept a potential sexual abuser at bay.

Anxiety may be at the heart of a child's soiling issues, particularly if his problems are inconsistent. Events in the present may trigger past feelings of abuse and neglect. Traumatized children are often hyper-vigilant and aware of nuances that are difficult to recognize. For example, a frown or slightly raised voice may trigger feelings of past abuse and neglect. Indeed, research has highlighted that traumatized children are more prone to seeing anger in a variety of facial expressions than non-traumatized children. It may, therefore, be difficult to recognize the triggers. A parent may have shouted upstairs to tell her child that dinner is ready, and this may have triggered fear in the child. A teacher may have raised her voice to ensure that she could be heard at the back of the class; again, this could trigger fear in a traumatized child. Recreating the familiar may also be a reason. The child may be so used to the smell and feel of pee and poo that he 'needs' to create these familiar smells to feel comfortable. This may be one of the reasons for a child either hiding soiled pants or smearing faeces. The child may also feel that he does not deserve to be clean and well cared for.

Confronting a child with his soiling problem may lead to feelings of overwhelming shame. Not being able to control his bladder and being aware that you disapprove may well mean that he seeks to hide the 'evidence'. The hiding of soiled pants is a significant problem for many parents of traumatized children.

Although it is difficult to address elimination issues, this does not mean that the child will continue to soil and wet. Using therapeutic parenting strategies in relation to other issues should help the child feel safer and more secure. This is likely to lead to a reduction in anxiety and therefore reduce the triggers that underlie the child's soiling problems.

Demonstrating empathy and understanding rather than frustration is crucial, as is the belief that the child can manage to be clean, with your help:

'I would struggle to be clean if I'd been hurt the way you have.'

'I think you're letting me know that you don't feel safe. Thanks for letting me know that. How about a cuddle to show you that I love you?'

'Do you know that I love you before and after your shower?'

Hiding soiled pants can be addressed by taking responsibility for the child's underwear. This might mean making the decision to give the child his underwear daily and supporting the placing of dirty underwear in the washing basket. This needs to be done in a non-shaming way: *'Because I know it's hard for you to manage, I'm going to help you with this.'* This will also provide the message that the child deserves a clean room and it begins to create the feeling that a soil-free environment is safe.

Schools can help by working with parents to find a co-ordinated approach to the child. Having spare pants and making sure that any 'accidents' are dealt with in a non-shaming way will also help.

SUMMARY

Thinking about pee and poo issues highlights the fact that, while you need to work to understand the underlying reasons for a child's difficulties, there are some behavioural presentations that are difficult to address directly.

Instead, you may need to 'park' certain issues while addressing some of the other behaviours presented by the child. This is not to imply that you need to excuse or accept certain behaviours that are causing difficulties for you and your child. Instead, it means recognizing that the child's behaviour allows you access to his inner 'language' in a variety of ways. Fear lies at the heart of this 'language'. Recognizing this means that you can work to help reduce the child's feelings of fear and insecurity by addressing a behaviour that is more readily manageable. You can do this in the knowledge that helping the child feel safer and less fearful is likely to have an impact on other fear-based behaviours.

This is akin to learning a new language. If your vocabulary is limited you may have to find a way of expressing your views in the vocabulary you have, while you work to increase your knowledge base.

Choosing your battles also means recognizing that you cannot tackle all difficulties at once. You may want to choose a maximum of two or three issues to address, ones that you feel most confident of helping the child with. When you begin to see positive change, you can build on your success to address more intractable issues.

PART 2
ACTION CHARTS

How to Use the Charts

The charts that feature in Part 2 are designed to be used as aide memoires to help in developing therapeutic parenting skills. They are also available online in A4 format so you can print off copies to pin on your wall. These can be downloaded from www.jkp.com/voucher using the code GORDONPARENT.

The tables consider some of the specific behaviour problems that many traumatized children display. I hope that some (but not all!) are relevant to your family situation.

Parenting a traumatized child can seem overwhelming at times, and I'd suggest that you choose the one or two behavioural issues most relevant for your family. Focusing on only one or two issues at a time should make the task of parenting more manageable.

As change occurs, you can move on to other issues. Indeed, you may find that other issues become less problematic. Children may 'speak' about their inner world in various behavioural ways. Addressing one aspect of 'behavioural language' may help your children 'speak' the language of safety and security rather than the language of fear and trauma.

Each behavioural issue is clearly defined and each chart and is laid out on facing pages. This format is designed to make it easier for you to quickly reference.

There is a blank chart at the end, and an editable copy online, which can be accessed through the link described above. Using the blank chart, you can personalize and tailor the material to your individual child.

As throughout the rest of the book, I have alternated between the use of 'he' and 'she' in our charts, and the blank chart will allow you to personalize the gender specificity.

Each chart looks at the developmental trauma issues. As I have highlighted, children's behaviour is often the only 'language' they have to express their inner fears and worries. It's important to remember this when you think about ways to interact with your children. While their behaviour may feel frustrating, remember that they're doing the best they can and their behaviour reflects their early experiences more than their relationship with you. It is a case of 'can't do', rather than 'won't do'. The executive functions involved in each behavioural issue are highlighted around the head in each chart. You may wish to refer to Part 1 to make sense of these executive functions.

Having said this, the charts also give the message that, with your help, change is possible. This is vital. Traumatized children often live in fear and feel a sense of hopelessness that they will ever feel safe and secure. They need not only your help to make the changes that will alter their inner feelings from ones that are fear based to ones that are based on safety and security, they also need your sense of hope that change is possible.

The charts also highlight the executive functioning issues that may be impacting traumatized children. These issues are, like attachment issues, an outcome of the early traumas the child experienced. Before you use the charts, try to think in as much detail as possible about not only what the child experienced, but also what it did to him. While painful, this will help you recognize the 'messages' your child received in his early months and years and assist you in developing the empathetic understanding of the underlying reasons for his difficulties. This is a crucial starting point. Understanding your children's inner world is the key to helping you to connect with them at an emotional level.

It's important to recognize that, while understanding and empathy need to be the cornerstone of your approach, you also need to provide your child with the message that certain behaviours are not acceptable. Understanding underlying reasons should not be used as an excuse for behaviour that negatively impacts family life and leaves your children 'fixed' in feelings that are unhealthy and do not allow them to begin to recover from their early traumas. One major task of parenting is to help children not only survive, but to thrive. Your children will not thrive unless they begin to feel that they are worthy of being helped to not only be safe but also to feel safe. The key to parenting, therefore, is to develop an approach that is based on nurture and structure.

There are no easy answers or quick fixes in parenting traumatized children. You are attempting to alter deep-seated fears and behaviours that emanate from your children's early experiences when the neurobiological patterns that underlie their beliefs were being formed. However, the charts should make your task a little bit easier.

While many of the suggested strategies focus on parenting issues, with minor adjustments they could be used to help children in school and in their wider community. A coherent and consistent approach not only supports parents in the difficult task they have undertaken in parenting their traumatized children, but also offers children the consistency they need to feel safer and more secure. The adage that 'it takes a village to raise a child' is relevant here.

Accepting Blame and Responsibility

👁 OBSERVED BEHAVIOUR

Aggression or seeming to 'switch off' and not listening when asked about something she has done.

Denying any involvement:
'You always blame me.'
'It's not fair.'
'It wasn't my fault.'
'I know nothing about it.'

😊 ATTACHMENT/ DEVELOPMENTAL TRAUMA ISSUE

Shame – your child may feel personally responsible for what has happened to her in the past; she may have been told that it was her fault or that it was what she wanted.

She may feel that her actions led to her being taken away or to others being punished.

'Bad' behaviour in her early life may have led to unwarranted physical punishment – fear may be driving her inability or refusal to accept blame for her actions.

What can I do?

Supervision will minimize misdemeanours. Adapt the environment to avoid negative behaviours.

Do not ask, *'Why did you do this?'* The child does not know the answer.

If you *know* she is responsible for the incident, then don't ask her, tell her: *'I know you took the money. I understand how difficult it was for you to stop yourself when you saw it.'*

Role play incidents after the event to show other ways of managing.

Practise apologizing when you make a mistake.

⚡ TRIGGER

Being reprimanded or expecting to be reprimanded for a misdemeanour. This may occur in situations when you are asking a question such as 'How was your day at school?' Your child might feel that this is an implied criticism, even if this is not your intention.

What can I do?

Pre-empt your child's potential feelings by acknowledging and validating the emotion she may be feeling, for example: *'I can see this is difficult for you. If I had been hurt the way you were hurt, I'd struggle to say that what happened was my fault.'* Or: *'I wonder if my telling you off makes you feel I don't love you?'*

Make consequences appropriate and ensure that they don't accentuate shame or feelings of abandonment.

Draw a line under the incident when the sanction has been implemented.

Your child will not cope with a 'three stikes and you're out' approach; it lacks the structure she needs.

Avoid confrontational situations and do not insist on eye contact.

To reduce shame, limit any reprimand to a ten-second scolding.

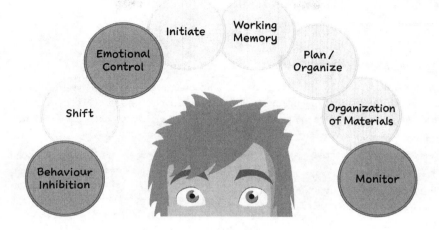

📖 FURTHER REFLECTIONS

You may also need to praise small achievements; for example, if she's started to clean the car, you can praise a clean wing mirror rather than waiting for her to complete the full task. If possible use humour: *'Thanks for cleaning the mirror, it allows me to check whether I'm still as beautiful as I was this morning.'*

If you know she struggles to accept responsibility, acknowledge this in advance of addressing the issue: *'I know you'll find it difficult but I need to talk to you about who took the money.'*

Your child needs boundaries and to accept that there are consequences when she has overstepped those boundaries. However, her emotional development is below that expected for her chronological age and she needs the adults in her life to be her 'external regulators', adapting her environment as one would for a toddler so that the possibility of failure is reduced.

You need to empathize with why she finds it difficult to acknowledge responsibility while also being clear about the consequences. She may need your help to manage the consequences; for example, if she has been asked to clean the car to repay stolen money you may have to help or supervize.

Acting the Victim

👁 OBSERVED BEHAVIOUR

Demonstrating fear of verbal or physical aggression from sibling, friend, classmate and so on that is greater than you would expect.

Seeming to invite reactive responses from others.

Some children display major upset over small hurts yet are impervious to major hurts.

Some children alternate between 'victim' and 'aggressor'.

😊 ATTACHMENT/ DEVELOPMENTAL TRAUMA ISSUE

Your child's early life history could have involved siblings competing for attention, food, nurture and so on, in order to survive, with a possibility that attention could have focused around sexual abuse. Siblings may have been the 'favourites' while your child was victimized or neglected.

Alternatively, your child might have been the 'favourite' and resents your attempts to treat your children more equally. Siblings could have been encouraged to be abusive towards each other. Aggressive relationships could have been set by the adults in their lives.

Your child may feel he is within his comfort zone, replicating his early environment. Your child may have very little self-esteem and could be feeling responsible for what has happened in the past, with the resultant shame.

What can I do?

Role play scenarios, helping your child find alternative responses. This could include role playing how to walk away. Help him to think about his emotions.

Use smiley face stickers to help him begin to desensitize himself – one colour for when he feels anxious, another colour when he feels sad. The differences between the two might help him to get his feelings into perspective.

Help him remember that he is now safe and with parents who can love all their children: *'I guess it's hard for you to remember that I love you when I'm paying attention to your sister.'*

💥 TRIGGER

Any setting where your child mixes with children whom he perceives as intimidating or threatening.

Situations where he feels he might gain attention or get a sibling into trouble.

Situations where your child is experiencing jealousy.

What can I do?

Children's safety (both physical and emotional) is the important issue here. Monitor the situation to ensure clarification of what is actually happening.

Validate your child's feelings: *'I know how difficult this is for you. The adults in your life will keep you safe.'*

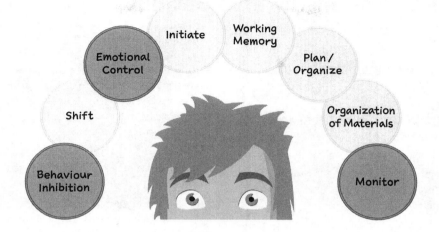

Avoid settings in which your child can become a victim; separate siblings within the home or monitor their behaviour.

Find opportunities to develop your child's self-esteem. Praise should be specific, especially if your child struggles with praise. Use games and activities to praise your child for specific actions: *'You kicked that ball really well'* rather than *'You're a great kid.'*

Provide opportunities for him to talk to you. He may need support to do this. Give him a token he can hand to you if he is worried.

📖 FURTHER REFLECTIONS

Children who have not had the opportunity to develop a primary attachment with their parents find it difficult to manage secondary attachments. Children who have suffered early developmental trauma often experience peer problems. Victimization can be real or imaginary, and it can be frustrating if it appears that your child courts aggression from others. It is important to recognize that the feelings are real to the child. His behaviour needs to be seen as his language, demonstrating possible anxiety and fear.

Let him know you understand this and can empathize with his difficulties. It might be helpful for you to respond to every hurt your child identifies. That way you may help fill the emotional gaps that are at the root cause of his behaviour and help your child to let go of the feelings that underlie it. Helping him to differentiate between 'big' hurts and 'little' hurts can also help, although this might have to be a secondary strategy.

Aggression Towards Siblings

👁 OBSERVED BEHAVIOUR

Sibling aggression.

😊 ATTACHMENT/DEVELOPMENTAL TRAUMA ISSUE

Survival strategy – fight. The 'fight' response along with 'flight' and 'freeze' are recognized survival responses to feelings of fear.

This child feels she alone is responsible for keeping herself safe; others have not managed to do this in the past.

She may have learned to employ an aggressive strategy to protect herself from violence or abuse, to protect others or even to claim food.

The need for control – she may have lost control early in her life; she may not be prepared to accept controlling behaviours from others.

Neurobiologically her body may be geared to produce high levels of stress-related hormones such as adrenaline and cortisol. Highly charged incidents allow her to release some of this.

What can I do?

If the child can talk about her feelings, try role playing incidents and practising appropriate reactive behaviours.

Talk about the body's physical state of anger so the child is able to recognize the early signs.

Give the child practical strategies to be angry in a more appropriate way; for example, writing her feelings rather than acting them out. You may need to be happy with whatever words your child uses to express her feelings, perhaps encouraging her to tear up her words as a way to get rid of her angry feelings.

Employ close supervision to avoid the possibility of incidents leading to aggression.

Use 'My Calming Poster' to emphasize the 'no hurting' rule. This can be downloaded from www.jkp.com/voucher using the code GORDONPARENT.

💥 TRIGGER

Inability to manage a perceived threat.

Disagreement with a sibling, accentuating a feeling of aloneness.

Losing a game, thus losing control.

Not being allowed to be in control of a game or activity.

Feeling that the sibling is favoured.

Feeling that attention given to a sibling means less attention for her.

What can I do?

Supervize sibling interactions in structured activities as a preventative approach rather than a sanction.

Verbalize your understanding of the child's difficulties.

Allow for supervized physical activity to burn off excess adrenaline and to practise playing safely.

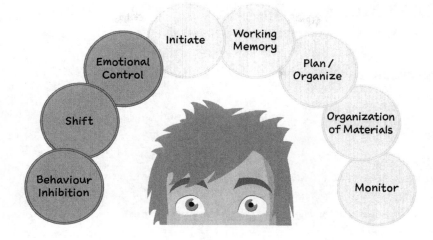

📖 FURTHER REFLECTIONS

You may find that most instances of aggression are displayed during unstructured and less-organized moments. This may be partly because your child feels unsafe in less supervized environments. Siblings can be wary of this child; some may act in ways that aggravate the situation; some may act out the role of 'victim' and seek out their sibling, even if this leads to being hurt. Use strategies to add more structure in settings that allow the behavior, and provide supervision at the times your child finds most difficult.

It is vital that the feelings behind the behaviour are acknowledged but it is also important to be clear that the behaviour is not acceptable. Your child needs to know that you can help him do things differently: *'You learned to be angry from people who didn't know safe ways of being angry. I can help you be angry in safe ways.'* Other siblings may need help with their role within the sibling relationship. It is not healthy to act out or practise being either abuser or victim.

Cheating at Games

👁 OBSERVED BEHAVIOUR

Cheating at games.

This is often linked to sibling rivalry and blaming others.

😊 ATTACHMENT/ DEVELOPMENTAL TRAUMA ISSUE

Need for control – your child may have unpleasant memories of when others controlled his life.

His need for control is crucial to him.

Shame – he feels immense shame for what has happened to him and his lack of self-worth leads to a need to 'prove himself'.

Survival strategy – your child may have needed to manipulate, 'cheat' or 'be the best' to keep alive and safe.

A fear of failure might feel life-threatening.

What can I do?

Validate your child's feelings: *'I know you find it hard to lose. I'm wondering how to help you know it's safe to lose sometimes.'*

Try to engineer situations where you can act as a role model for how to manage emotions if your child does not play fairly.

Help your child 'practise' losing and feeling okay about this: *'I love you whether you win or lose this game? How about losing so I can give you a cuddle just so you know.'*

Help your child reflect on the impact on siblings: *'It's hard for your sister when you cheat. I'll give her a cuddle to help her feel better about this.'*

💥 TRIGGER

Fear of failure.

Concern that losing a game means loss of control.

Children who struggle with self-esteem issues might feel that losing means they are a failure.

What can I do?

Remind the child with a statement before the game: *'I know how important it is to you to win at games. Can we think what you can do if you don't win this time?'*

Ensure the game is appropriate to your child's ability so that he can succeed without cheating.

Remember that your child may not be able to process all the instructions or may not have the skills and knowledge to play the game according to how it should be played.

Role play scenarios where your child loses and teach him strategies or mantras he can use in this situation: *'This is not a big deal. I may win another time.'*

Provide him with a vocabulary he can use, such as: *'Well done. Thank you for playing with me.'* He doesn't need to feel good about losing; he may need to practise the words in the hope the feelings follow.

If he can't use the words, mirror what he should say by saying it for him.

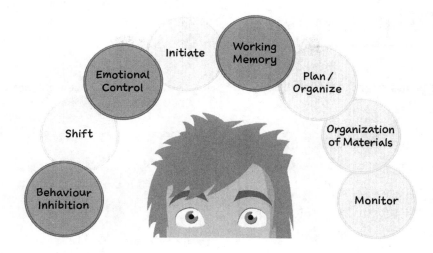

Many of these children have difficulty managing peer or sibling relationships, and cheating at games is likely to inflame these relationships further. There are many games available commercially that are not competitive and that might help your child to engage with others in a non-competitive way. You could even make up games where you win by losing, such as a slow walking competition. The aim should be to help your child feel good about himself whether he wins or loses so that he no longer feels that he needs to win to survive.

This should also help the child's feelings of self-esteem. While you might want to ensure that your child always wins as this reduces tensions, this does not really provide a good learning opportunity.

Instead, he needs to practise winning *and* losing and recognizing that this is not a life-threatening experience. Talk in advance about what he might do instead of his usual response to losing. Role play these alternatives in a fun way, at times that are not linked to the specific game; for example, while out for a walk or when you are driving. Remember to praise your child when he loses if he has managed the feelings better than before: *'Well done. I noticed you stamped your feet. Usually you would have thrown the game at me. Maybe you're learning how to manage the disappointment of losing.'*

Completing Tasks

👁 OBSERVED BEHAVIOUR

Refusal to undertake reasonable requests by parent.

Agreeing to a request but then not doing it.

Beginning a task but not completing it.

😊 ATTACHMENT/ DEVELOPMENTAL TRAUMA ISSUE

Shame – anxiety about getting it wrong may be overwhelming.

Your child may have lived in an environment where she was in a constant state of fear.

She may have been blamed for her and others' actions.

She may feel an overwhelming sense of responsibility for what has happened to her and others close to her.

She may be struggling to know where and how to begin.

The task might feel overwhelming.

She may have been used to chaos.

An untidy room might reflect her inner chaos.

Fear of failure might feel life threatening.

What can I do?

Validate her feelings: *'I know you find starting tasks difficult. I can see you worry about being wrong. I can help you with this.'*

Provide support at the start and during the task.

Talk through what the task entails, breaking this into manageable chunks.

A pictorial representation of the task might help. Find ways to praise parts of the task your child has managed to complete, even if she doesn't finish the whole task.

💥 TRIGGER

Being given a new task.

Being asked to tidy her room, or a similar task.

The feeling of pressure of being expected to carry out a task can lead to tantrums and arguments.

Being asked to engage in a rota of tasks; this is likely to cause arguments of 'it's not my turn'.

What can I do?

Chunk the work, asking your child to complete and show her work in parts.

Provide a schema or format for work, in written or picture format.

Use simple, explicit instructions.

Consider working alongside her and repeating the next instruction as your child works.

Suggest that after completing her task you both work together on one of yours.

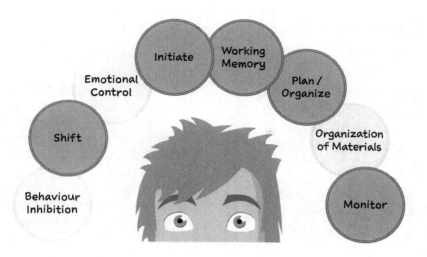

📖 FURTHER REFLECTIONS

Your child is not lazy, and would probably love to complete tasks with ease. Asking her to do something may provide extra anxiety and fears she cannot manage. You need to recognize and validate this. For example, if you ask her to tidy her room: *'I guess you might be worried about how to go about tidying your room. I can understand this. Why don't you start with putting your socks in the laundry basket? Then we can work out what to do next.'* Or: *'When you were little nobody kept you clean and tidy. Your room lets me know you still don't feel you deserve to be clean and tidy. I can help you practise feeling that you deserve to be looked after. Let's start by putting the socks in the laundry basket and then I can help you with what to do next.'*

Or: *'I know you find this hard so I've taken a picture of your room when it's tidy and here's a list of what you need to do to get it looking like this. Let me know if you need help.'*

Sitting with her while she completes the task might help her regulate and be able to think through the task better. While this might feel like a waste of your time, it is likely that the time spent will be less than you going back repeatedly to ensure the task is completed. You could get your child to help you with one of your tasks as helping her has left you short of time. Doing things together, including tasks, can provide opportunities for attachment and relationship building: two crucial things that your child needs help with.

Compliant and Helpful

👁 OBSERVED BEHAVIOUR

Your child may rarely present problematic or disruptive behaviour and is often not considered to have any problems. He is reported to be helpful and reliable and trying hard.

Other people are likely to comment on how well he is managing in spite of his past.

Your experience of him is likely to be very different: he may act out his distress with you or seem to prefer others to you.

😊 ATTACHMENT/ DEVELOPMENTAL TRAUMA ISSUE

Under this people-pleasing behaviour, there probably lies an incredibly anxious child who is desperate to please to avoid further rejection.

Keeping up this act requires boundless energy and can be draining. For some of these youngsters, it is not until later in life that they can analyse their early behaviours, and their knowledge of living a lie can lead to depression.

Often these children act out differently with parents who experience the 'emptiness' of the child. Their experience is that this child is like a 'lodger' in their home. Often the child will be indiscriminately friendly with comparative strangers. It is important to accept your gut instincts about your child and seek help for him.

What can I do?

The inner struggle to control his feelings needs to be recognized. Try to lessen the pressure for him to behave well at all times.

You might want to help him to practise being 'naughty'; for example, tearing up paper together, leaving a mess. This may help him see that bad behaviour does not equate with rejection of the person.

You could role model being 'naughty'. Perhaps by having a day off from usual chores. Make sure to let your child know how naughty you have been and 'forgive' yourself for your naughtiness.

💥 TRIGGER

Everyday living will result in this compliancy.

Any sign your child interprets as a possible rejection.

Having a sibling who is angry and overtly acting out.

What can I do?

These children need to know they will still be accepted whatever their behaviour. Give specific praise and accept some offers of help but discourage others: *'That's good of you to offer but I think you need to practise letting me doing this for you just now.'* Or: *'I think you need to practise being a child right now.'*

If there is a lapse in behaviour, try to accept it and don't be tempted to say: *'Well I thought you knew better than that. I thought I could rely on you.'*

Although sounding contrary to expectations, it might be appropriate to be pleased about 'bad' behaviour as it may signal that he is feeling secure enough to demonstrate his anxieties.

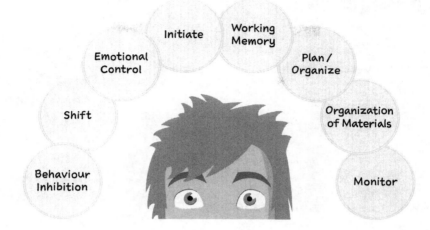

FURTHER REFLECTIONS

Often, assessments of these children's executive skills show good control in most situations. Their scores on assessment questionnaires do not appear in the clinically high range, or present in the clinically low range. This makes it even harder for others to see the child's difficulties, and parents can feel isolated and alone.

Some compliant children are able to control their behaviour at home as well as at school. If this is not addressed, they can experience problems later in life. However, it may well be that your child displays completely contrasting behaviour at home. He may seem to change dramatically even as he walks out of school to meet you.

You may be struggling to contain challenging behaviour and his compliant behaviour at school may add to your feelings of rejection and failure. You may feel that staff at school do not believe you or consider you to be 'bad parents'. You need professionals who can see your child's underlying difficulties, show an understanding of the situation and offer support and empathy.

Consequences

👁 OBSERVED BEHAVIOUR

Struggling to accept consequences of behaviour decided by parents.

Arguing about consequences of misdemeanours.

Not agreeing to go to her room when asked.

😊 ATTACHMENT/ DEVELOPMENTAL TRAUMA ISSUE

Fear – she may be afraid she will not be able to manage her emotions, and frightened that these could escalate out of control. If the consequence involves isolation, the isolation could trigger traumatic memories of early neglect.

Shame – your child may feel responsible for the trauma in her early life. She may be struggling to manage her behaviour and is further shamed by the consequence.

Control – she may feel a need to be in control and not to be subject to parameters set by adults.

Developmental trauma can impact a child's sensory development. She may become over-stimulated by a busy environment and be unable to remember what was asked of her.

What can I do?

Validate her feelings, for example: *'I know you find it difficult to do as I ask. Let's see if I can help you with this.'*

Give children 'time in' rather than 'time out'.

Remember, consequences that involve an expectation for her to manage independently when she is feeling dysregulated can ignite further dysregulation. She needs a supportive adult to be with her.

💥 TRIGGER

A conversation, a perception of injustice, a disappointment, an argument and so on.

A fear of rejection, reprimand, isolation.

Struggling to accept parental control.

Feeling out of control.

Feeling shame for actions that led to the consequence.

What can I do?

If the problem that is leading to there being a consequence is connected to remembering or planning, the use of external cues can help – for example, alarms on watches, telephones. Your child may need reminding to set alarms.

It can be helpful to run through a visualization technique, imagining the task and how she might manage to perform it.

If your child does not want to make the shift from what she is doing, validate this: *'I can see you probably don't want to leave your friends, but you do need to do...'*

It is always better to help your child succeed than to impose a consequence for failure.

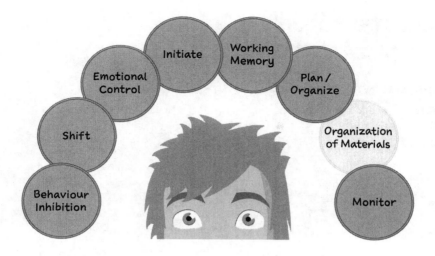

The issue of consequences is a difficult one for many families. Parents have a natural expectation that their child will adhere to reasonable requests and parameters and it is frustrating when there are constant battles over the minutia of family life. While all children need boundaries and to know that behaviour that crosses these boundaries is unacceptable, there is also a need for disciplinary procedures to be consistent and fair.

The consequence should be appropriate to the deed and there must be an understanding that your child may struggle to keep within the boundaries, not because she is being purposely defiant, but because her early trauma is triggering a defensive reaction. If your child is constantly struggling with tasks that are within her capacities, it possibly demonstrates that the consequences you are using are not working for her and that perhaps other interventions need to be implemented to support her.

Remembering that this may a case of 'can't do' not 'won't do' should help you to consider whether your child needs extra support. This may be the case when she can complete a task one day and not another; it may be that an event in the present is triggering an early trauma memory and that this is reducing your child's ability to manage or to feel good about herself. Recognizing this for yourself as well as your child is likely to reduce tension and frustration. The aim should always be to provide opportunities that help your child succeed rather than fail. This means that, while you need to adhere to boundaries, you might need to be creative in the way you help her manage the boundary and the feelings this engenders. 'Three strikes and you're out' strategies are not likely to work as your child may interpret this as you being inconsistent.

Constant Fiddling

👁 OBSERVED BEHAVIOUR

Fiddling continuously with shoes, clothing, furniture and so on.

Struggling to sit still.

☺ ATTACHMENT/ DEVELOPMENTAL TRAUMA ISSUE

This could be part of ADHD behaviour.

It could be due to sensory arousal.

Many traumatized children live in a constant state of anxiety, sometimes not even feeling the security that they will be returning to the same home after school.

Their constant need to be 'on the move' could hide anxiety.

Fiddling can be a way to use up excess adrenaline, levels of which may be heightened due to early life experiences.

Constant fiddling might be a defence against intrusive thoughts and feelings.

What can I do?

Try to alleviate any anxieties your child may have; for example, give warning of changes to routine.

Build lots of short physical breaks into your family routine.

Incorporate more kinaesthetic learning opportunities (i.e. doing activities rather than listening or watching demonstrations).

Allow him to 'doodle' if necessary.

💥 TRIGGER

Anxiety about what is coming next.

Separation anxiety.

Sensory issues – your child may have an allergy to certain materials.

What can I do?

Accept your child's need to fiddle and work with it.

Provide him with a suitable fiddling toy – one that won't make a noise, roll away or be dangerous to others. It needs to be something you are content with, and you need to feel at ease with him doing this, remembering that he may well have to use his toy at family times like mealtimes.

Suggest other ways to use up excess adrenaline, such as doing star jumps.

Empathize with the potential underlying reasons for your child's difficulties.

📖 FURTHER REFLECTIONS

Remember that your child is not likely to know what is going on with him, so don't expect an answer. What is important is that he feels your empathy and your attempts to help. The fiddling might be more prevalent after he has been separated all day from you at school or when he is asked to go to bed. Children are expected to be quiet in bed in preparation for sleep. In these quiet periods, intrusive thoughts and feelings may emerge. Exploring this with your child may help, as will validating his feelings and offering suggestions about what he might do differently, for example having a mantra

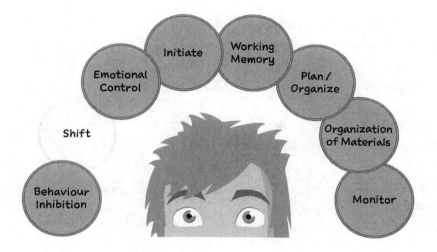

that he can repeat: *'I'm safe, even when I'm keeping still and quiet.'*

You might also like to suggest short periods in which you're both 'practising' managing anxious feelings without fiddling. Here it is important not to ask your child not to feel anxious; instead you should give him permission to feel anxious and suggest ways that, with your help, he can manage this.

Gradually these feelings are likely to diminish; as he becomes able to tolerate feelings of anxiety he will see that there is little need for these feelings. Expect this to take time and recognize that at times of increased stress, these feelings might re-emerge. This is natural and not a sign of failure.

While fiddling may be a sign of anxiety, it is important to rule out or in other factors. Diet may play a part. Consider referring your child for a clinical dietary assessment; even if you have a healthy diet your child's early experience may be interfering with his ability to benefit from this. Your child may also be helped by a referral

to a paediatric occupational therapist, who will assess any sensory difficulties and can provide exercises to help. The occupational therapist might also suggest materials you could buy.

You might want to consider whether there are any other reasons for your child's difficulties, such as ADHD. You could ask your GP for a referral to assess this.

It is important to consider any specific times of the day when the fiddling is worse. If this is linked to separation issues, the difficulties might be more prevalent in the morning before school. In this instance, it is important to validate your child's feelings: *'I've noticed you start fiddling every morning. I wonder if, inside, you are feeling anxious about what will happen next. I guess I would feel like that if I had had the number of changes you've had in your life. If you feel anxious at school you can use your toy, or you might want to look at the family photo in your school bag to remind you that I will be picking you up from school. Do you know that I often look at your photo and think about you when you're at school?'*

Dangerous Behaviour

👁 OBSERVED BEHAVIOUR

Dangerous and irresponsible behaviour – either to himself or others.

These children often elicit anxiety and fear in others.

☺ ATTACHMENT/ DEVELOPMENTAL TRAUMA ISSUE

Your child may not have experienced a normal toddlerhood; he may have been exposed to an unsafe environment without parental supervision.

This experience may have led to an inability to perceive danger or the need to keep 'safe'.

He may have little or no concept of cause and effect.

Shame could lead to putting himself in situations where he may get hurt 'purposely'.

Control – he may have a need to demonstrate that he has control over his life. If he feels he has control over his actions this lessens the feeling that he needs to rely on other people.

He may not feel good about himself, which could engender self-harming behaviour.

Fear underpins dangerous and irresponsible behaviour.

What can I do?

Your child needs the adults in his life to act as his external regulators. Verbalize the need to keep safe and involve him in thinking about tactics to keep himself safe. Talk through these so that he can start internalizing them: 'I love you enough to help you be safe.'

Practise safe behaviours with him. Video him when he is acting safely and talk him through the safety aspects as you watch it with him.

Be a role model. Using your mobile when driving, for example, is not being a good role model for your child.

💥 TRIGGER

Feeling insecure or unsafe.

A memory from the past, possibly subconscious.

A lack of attention from adults.

If this is a control issue, the knowledge that adults consider safety important.

A fear-based response.

Self-harming behaviours.

A need to discharge adrenaline.

What can I do?

Your child needs to be kept safe and so the environment needs to be adapted to enable this.

Speak to him about the worry his behaviour causes and the need for you to keep him safe: 'I know that when you were a baby, adults didn't keep you safe. I need to help you learn how to keep safe. We could practise... together so that I can keep you safe.' Or: 'We are the adults in your life and we need to keep you safe, so we are not allowing you on...until we can figure out how you can use it safely.'

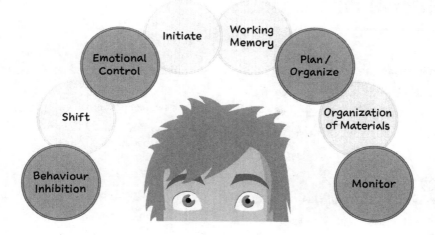

Think 'toddler' and ensure that your child is constantly monitored, with the environment modified to allow this. *'I'm glad you're giving me the chance to look after you; I didn't get the chance to do this when you were a baby.'*

Offer less risky alternatives to the dangerous behaviour.

📖 FURTHER REFLECTIONS

Obviously, a dangerous situation needs to be stopped immediately but safely. Your child may not comprehend, for example, that the quickest way down from a height is probably not the safest! Try to make your interventions non-shaming. For example, making your child watch other children having fun in the pool is shaming. Instead, you might consider going with him into the pool and role playing safe pool behaviour.

If that's not possible try statements like: *'I can see you are struggling to keep yourself and others safe just now so you need to sit with me while we work this out.'* Your child is behaving in this manner because of the impact of his past life history. It is important to empathize with this while, at the same time giving the message that the behaviour is not okay.

Whatever his outward presentation, beneath the bravado is a scared child who wants others to keep him safe until he can do this himself.

If self-harming is an issue: *'I'm sad you don't feel good enough about yourself to practise safe behaviour. I'm wondering what I can do to help you feel better about yourself?'* Self-harming produces a chemical reaction in the body that anesthetizes against emotion pain.

You need to be able to talk about difficult feelings and offer alternative ways to manage them. Just removing the knives, for example, won't ensure your child's safety.

Disrupting Others

👁 OBSERVED BEHAVIOUR

Inability to focus on her own activity.

Disrupting what siblings are doing.

Curiosity about sibling's activities.

Interfering with a sibling's game.

😊 ATTACHMENT/ DEVELOPMENTAL TRAUMA ISSUE

Need for hyper-vigilance – a survival strategy learned as a baby. Attention or food given to a sibling might have exposed this child to trauma.

Feeling that you prefer another child.

Your child 'needs' to know what is going on and is unable to focus on one activity when there is another activity around her.

She may also have difficulty if asked to choose between activities as she will not want to 'miss out' on one activity for another.

Control issues – a need to be able to manage everything.

The 'buzz' in the house, which reminds the child of previous difficult situations.

Re-enactment of an early trauma bond.

What can I do?

Provide adult intervention to refocus your child.

She may need to sit near you.

Help your child to plan the task and perhaps remain with her while she begins.

Provide a timer so your child knows how long this activity will last.

Support her at the beginning and end of each task.

Validate her feelings verbally.

Closely monitor your children when they are playing together.

💥 TRIGGER

Separate activities provided for each child.

Children being encouraged to share and play together.

Thinking her sibling is getting more love or attention.

Being unsure of what everyone else is doing.

Jealousy.

What can I do?

Empathize with your child's difficulties and validate her need to know all that is going on – 'I know it's hard for you to share with your sister and it's also hard for you to see your sister playing by herself.' Or: 'I can see you find it hard to focus on your own activity.' Or: 'I can see you're worried about what your sister is doing.'

Show your child what her siblings are doing to satisfy her need.

Limit choices and help her to choose if necessary: 'I've looked out a special activity for you today.'

Remind your child that you are a parent who can love all your children.

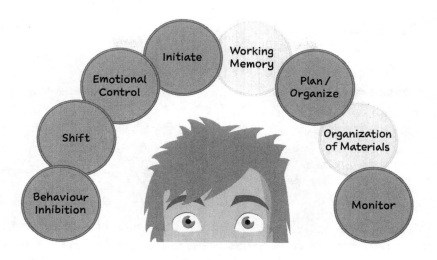

📖 FURTHER REFLECTIONS

Developmental trauma often impacts on the sensory development of these children. Many demonstrate problems in focusing and are easily distracted by other things that are going on in the family. Often bedrooms are filled with a plethora of games and toys. Some children can find this too stimulating and may benefit from having an area that is less 'busy'. Although your child may need to work on her own at times, one aim is to encourage sibling interaction at a manageable level. Your child may need help to 'practise' this. This must not be presented as a punishment and care may have to be taken to ensure your child does not feel rejected. *'I know you find it hard to be with your sister. You never got a chance to practise being together safely when you were little. We're going to practise playing safely for five minutes. I'll sit with you while we practise.'*

It's important that you choose the sibling time carefully; choose the number of minutes you know your children can manage and suggest two minutes less; that way she can experience success rather than failure. If you allow your children to play together only to remove one child when she is struggling, she will experience this as failure regardless of how this is presented.

Similarly, it's better for your child to join at the end rather than the beginning of individual activity so that when the activity ends both children feel that this is 'fair'. Your child will benefit from adult attention and this should place her more in a position to manage.

Focusing on a Task

👁 OBSERVED BEHAVIOUR

Lack of focus.

Inability to begin or complete a task. This may involve nonsense chatter, fiddling, aimless behaviour, copying or interfering with others, or just sitting doing nothing.

Staring into space.

😊 ATTACHMENT/ DEVELOPMENTAL TRAUMA ISSUE

Shame – anxiety about being wrong. As a baby your child may have been in a constant state of fear.

He may have been blamed for his and others' actions. He may feel an overwhelming sense of responsibility for what has happened to him and those close to him.

Need for hyper-vigilance – a survival strategy learned as a baby. Although he is not threatened by you he may feel as if he is and 'needs' to know what is going on, so he is unable to focus.

Developmental trauma can impact on a child's sensory development. He may become over-stimulated by a busy environment and be unable to cope.

Neurobiologically, your child's processing skills may have been affected.

What can I do?

Validate his feelings, for example: *'I know you find starting and sticking to tasks difficult. I can see you worry about being wrong. I can help you with this.'*

Provide support at the start and during the task.

Check regularly and offer praise for what he has managed. *'Well done you've put your socks in the laundry basket. I'll come back in five minutes and check on the t-shirt.'*

💥 TRIGGER

Being given a task, such as tidy your room.

Being given several or complex instructions.

Asking a sibling to do something.

Feeling that there are expectations placed on him (whether stated or not).

What can I do?

Chunk the work, asking your child to complete and show what he's done in parts.

'It's time for tidying your room. Why don't you start with your books and then go on to tidy your toys?'

Use simple explicit instructions, giving only one or two instructions at a time, and be prepared to help: *'Great, books are on the shelf, toys are in their box; now let's think about the clothes. Can you find all the socks that need washing while I search for the t-shirts?'*

Use visual reminders, such as a photo of each of the things that need to be put away and what a tidy room looks like.

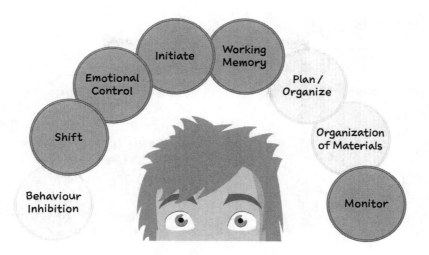

📖 FURTHER REFLECTIONS

Your child is not lazy, and would probably love to be able to complete tasks. However, the complexity of the task may overwhelm him. Tidying a room is a task that requires a complex set of procedures that might confuse your child. Working alongside your child might help him to see what is required and you can also act as a good role model. Providing a list of the elements of the task with appropriate pictures might help.

A tick sheet may help your child to remember what is expected of him.

Build in breaks: *'Once you've found five dirty socks we can have a cuddle.'* Be encouraging, rather than reprimanding: *'Great, three socks – well done, let's go and find another two.'*

Try to build in humour: *'Do you think that sock's partner might be in the alternative sock universe; or perhaps it's sulking? When we find it, I'm going to ask.'*

Older children may have to accept the consequences of not completing tasks: *'Friday is tidying room day; feel free to tidy your room or pay me to do it for you.'* Here you need to be happy with your child's choice and if you tidy the room be happy with the flowers you buy with your earnings. Offer to help your child on the understanding that he helps you with your tasks.

If your tasks are more time consuming and less pleasant this might be an incentive for your child to complete his tasks. If you do help your child, try to look at this as an opportunity to develop attachments. You can share this with him: *'Thanks for letting me help you today. I really enjoyed the opportunity to talk to you while we worked. Let's see if we can talk above the noise of the vacuum cleaner while we clean the kitchen.'*

Food Issues

👁 OBSERVED BEHAVIOUR

Hiding food, hoarding food.

Eating others' food.

Not eating lunch and other meals.

Fussy eating.

Eating inappropriately, for example only one type of food.

Never feeling full and always asking for extra.

Liking food one day and hating it the next.

☺ ATTACHMENT/ DEVELOPMENTAL TRAUMA ISSUE

There are many possibilities for food issues.

Your child may have experienced extreme hunger or have suffered an inadequate or ill-balanced diet.

She may have had to fight others for food or eaten non-food objects. She may have undergone periods of food poisoning due to poor food hygiene practices. She may be unused to the type of food on offer.

She may see food issues as a way of maintaining control over her life. Eating disorders are often a way of coping with difficult feelings.

She may equate food with love.

Food might have been offered as a 'reward' for sexual abuse.

What can I do?

Involve her in considering strategies to help her.

Create a phrase that can be repeated to her until she can internalize it. *'There is always enough food in this house.'*

Place a daily menu on the fridge of the food, which also gives the timing of meals.

Offer a cuddle prior to meals to ensure she feels 'full' of love before eating.

Provide a menu with a tick list for children who are faddy or inconsistent.

💥 TRIGGER

Any occasion where food is involved.

Feeling unloved.

Equating food with filling emotional gaps.

Sibling rivalry.

Fear that there will never be enough (of anything).

Worry about where the next meal is coming from.

Any situation where the child feels out of control.

Self-harming.

What can I do?

Analyze the situation to define the true nature of the difficulty: *'I think a cuddle might fill the hole in your heart better than food.'*

Validate her feelings: *'I know this is difficult for you. I'm here to support you.'*

Help her to practise other ways of managing: *'Why don't you practise leaving just your peas?'*

Eat pudding first to give your child a message that the treat is the healthy food!

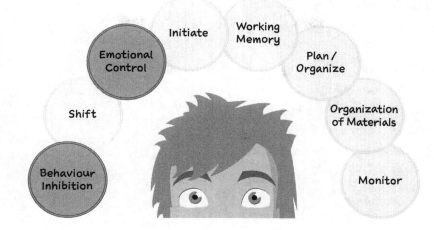

Liaise with the school to ensure food issues are dealt with appropriately.

Don't get into battles about your child feeling her brother is getting more.

📖 FURTHER REFLECTIONS

School lunchtimes can be traumatizing for a child. Work with the school to ensure that your child's eating environment reflects her needs; consider whether packed lunches or school meals are most appropriate. It may be necessary to seek the advice of a clinical dietician to ensure that your child has the optimal menu that reflects her history.

Help your child know you understand why food is such an issue: *'If I had not had enough food when I was a baby I would worry about what was for dinner.'*

Sibling issues around food are not ones you can win; you won't be able to convince your children that you are being fair. Instead use empathy: *'I guess I would struggle to know I had enough if I'd been hungry as a baby.'*

Don't use food as a control issue; this is *not* a battle you can win. If your child doesn't eat, try not to show how worried you are. Try to find ways of offering food in a fun and non-stressful way. Try to consider the underlying reasons for the problem and work on these in an empathetic way; this may help to reduce the need to use food to mask underlying traumas. You might need to consider your own feelings around food. You're not being a 'bad' parent if your child refuses to eat healthy food – it's to do with her past.

Food issues need to be handled carefully. Serious food issues may need trained medical support and assistance.

Homework Issues

👁 OBSERVED BEHAVIOUR

Not doing homework.

Having major arguments about homework.

Refusing to start homework.

Saying there is no homework when there is.

Not handing in homework.

🙂 ATTACHMENT/ DEVELOPMENTAL TRAUMA ISSUE

Control, especially if she knows this is important to you. This need for control possibly arises from a time when she had no control and suffered.

A feeling that what she achieves will not be good enough.

She may not have any internalized belief in the importance of education – she has no incentive to complete this work.

The need to bring homework home might pale into insignificance for children who feel they are fighting to survive and feel safe and secure.

Fear – of reprisals, reprimands and consequences.

Shame – feeling responsible for what has happened in the past. She may have been told that it was her fault or that it was what she wanted. She might feel that failure to live up to your or her teacher's expectations is further proof of her inherent 'badness'.

She feels 'rubbish' and has an inner feeling that what she achieves will not be good enough.

What can I do?

Work with teachers to establish the essential work and concentrate on this. Chunk extended work into manageable sections.

Encourage your child to attend homework facilities at school where she can be assisted by staff in a controlled, but supportive, environment.

Avoid constant reprimands for incomplete or non-existent homework as this adds to your child's feeling of shame and your frustration; work with teachers to ensure they know your child's difficulties and can take this into consideration.

If your child has attachment issues this should take priority. Don't insist on homework if this interferes with attachment.

If she struggles to hand in homework, consider making a copy and sending it to school.

💥 TRIGGER

Parental or teacher expectation of achievement, which threatens her view of herself as a failure or which she 'knows' she will fail to achieve.

Being asked to do homework.

Being asked to hand in homework.

The fear of failure.

Control issues – homework may be more of an issue for parents than for the child. Refusing to do homework can put your child in control.

Feeling that completing homework tasks are a priority for you.

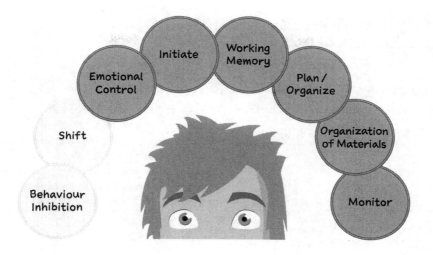

What can I do?

You might need to take more responsibility for helping your child organize her homework and you may have to closely monitor your child's work.

Try to provide a distraction free area, sit with your child, agree a time limit and stick to this. If she doesn't work, don't try to insist she does. You can't force her to do homework so don't try. When the time is up, put the work away reminding her she will have another amount of time tomorrow. Then move on to another activity.

You cannot make your child do homework; your job is to provide support and the environment she needs.

Negotiate with the school to ensure that homework comes home.

📖 FURTHER REFLECTIONS

The homework issue can be a source of major frustration for parents and can impact parent–child relationships.

Homework may not be a crucial issue for your child, especially if it requires huge control battles to ensure she completes it. Your priority is to foster attachments, and control battles around homework may be counter productive to this. Communicate with teachers to ensure they are aware of her difficulties and support you in helping her. She may display a defensive, uncaring exterior but it is important that she sees that you and the school are working together to support her. If you are more worried about her homework than she is, she is more likely to use this as a control issue. Support your child, but try not to see it as crucial to how effective you are as a parent.

Hypochondriac Tendencies

👁 OBSERVED BEHAVIOUR

Complaining constantly of minor ailments.

Often children who get very upset over minor things will be impervious to major hurts or accidents.

😊 ATTACHMENT/ DEVELOPMENTAL TRAUMA ISSUE

If the behaviour happens in school it could be linked to a hope that your child will be sent home. A need to return home is likely to stem from anxiety about something in school, something at home or possibly anxiety about rejection and abandonment.

They may be 'ill' to gain reassurance that you care. Some children who cannot express their feelings overtly will use 'illness' to express their inner feelings.

What can I do?

Use your knowledge of your child's history to figure out what he is telling you. Be curious about your child's inner feelings: *'I wonder if this is really about...'*

Accept that your child's stomach ache is real (to him): *'Gosh, I can see you're really not feeling great at the moment. I wonder if a cuddle might help.'*

Remind your child that you will be collecting him from school as a way of providing reassurance. A photograph or memento of home will also help.

💥 TRIGGER

Triggers could range from a variety of concerns, such as an inability to understand instructions, tasks they feel unable to complete, or a smell, sound, word, picture that produces a traumatic memory. These feelings are transferred into physical ailments.

Your child could be signalling an inner feeling that he cannot express overtly.

What can I do?

Try to warn your child of any impending change and be reassuring.

Act as a role model. Verbalize instances when you feel anxious and suggest strategies you use to calm yourself.

Validate your child's underlying feeling: *'I guess if I was really hurting inside I might have stomach pains.'*

Allow your child a special routine for coming into school so the teacher can be alerted if he is experiencing anxiety.

📖 FURTHER REFLECTIONS

If your child becomes accustomed to 'using' health issues to deal with emotional problems this could have long-term mental health consequences. It is vital that he is helped to address his feelings openly and get help to deal with these. However, you might want to use your child's 'illnesses' for a time to enhance attachments. This is especially relevant if your child has gone through a period of being impervious to

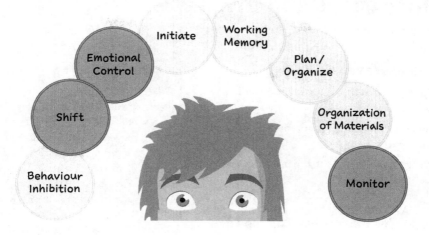

hurts, a 'strategy' some children have developed to manage early trauma.

In this situation, becoming upset over minor hurts might be a step on the road to repair. Having found ways to guard against experiencing pain he might find it hard to assess what is and is not a minor hurt. It might also be that, once your child can experience pain he needs to 'practise' this in minor pains while major hurts are still too overwhelming. It might also be a way of testing your love for him. In this situation, attending to your child's hurts both physically (a plaster) and emotionally (cuddles) is likely to help him.

School policy will dictate the circumstances for sending children home; no teacher wants an ill child in their class. This might be right in some situations but not always. Work with your child's teacher on strategies to manage your child's problems. Your child may be demonstrating his needs and extra time at home may help to improve attachments; however, this needs to be dictated by the adults rather than the child. This may be especially important if your child has siblings also vying for your attention. Use this time to develop your child's attachment to you; find books and strategies that will help foster attachment and experiment with those that work for you and your child. As your child's attachment increases you can begin to help him assess whether, on a scale of 1–10 this is a 'small' hurt or a 'big' hurt.

Intense Sibling Rivalry

👁 OBSERVED BEHAVIOUR

Verbal or physical aggression towards a sibling.

Intense tale-telling about a sibling or fear of a sibling.

Seeking out the sibling, perhaps in the context of 'helping'.

😊 ATTACHMENT/ DEVELOPMENTAL TRAUMA ISSUE

Your child's early life history could have involved siblings competing for attention, food and nurture in order to survive.

There is a possibility that attention could have focused around sexual abuse.

One sibling could have been the 'favourite' while others were victimized or neglected.

The children could have been encouraged to be abusive towards each other.

Aggressive relationships could have been the example set by adults in their lives.

What can I do?

The safety of all family members must take priority.

Children should not play unsupervized.

Use monitors when the children are in bedrooms. Have a no-entry rule to a sibling's bedroom – even with permission from the sibling. Some children will 'invite' their siblings into their room even if it's potentially dangerous or unhelpful; for example, children who assume the victim role may need help to change that role; children who assume the aggressor role also need help to change. And some siblings move between aggressor and victim.

Be available to talk things over if the children need to. Provide them with an item to give you if they wish to talk, or use a toy for them to talk through: *'I can see how difficult it is for you to let me know that you are worried. If you leave your teddy on the chair, I will know that you have a worry that you want to talk about.'* Or: *'I wonder what teddy might feel about this?'* You could also talk to teddy about what you might like to say to your child: *'Hi teddy (your child's name) I really want to let you know that I've noticed…'*

Give reassurance to a child who is afraid of his sibling: *'I know you worry about being hurt. We are going to help you be and feel safe.'*

💥 TRIGGER

At home: any time the children are together unsupervized.

Children being asked to share or play games together.

In school: incidents prior to arrival at school, home time, playtimes, whole-school occasions, settings where two classes mix, such as paired reading, shared 'news' reminding pupil of an earlier incident.

What can I do?

Set clear ground rules about what acceptable and non-acceptable ways to act in your family.

Role play possible scenarios to explore alternative responses. This could be done by adults acting as the children.

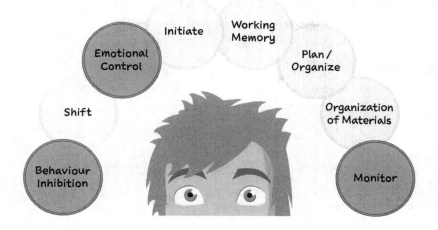

Remind children of your expectations of behaviour before they meet up: *'I know how hard it is for you when we all play together. We are going to practise five minutes playing together to help you play safely.'*

📖 FURTHER REFLECTIONS

Although it may appear that one child is the perpetrator, be aware that each sibling is actually a victim. The behaviour of the abusive sibling is her language, demonstrating her anxiety and unhappiness.

It is important to be honest about this child's behaviour in a non-shaming way: *'I know you sometimes hit your brother. I guess you learned to do this when you were little. I can help you be with your brother in a different way. This will help you feel better about yourself and keep your brother safe. Each day we will practise this together; meanwhile, children are not allowed to play together unless I am there and you are not allowed in your brother's bedroom even if he says it's okay.'* You may have to be proactive in leading family discussions about safety and appropriate behaviour.

You need to be vigilant and not expect the victim to take the lead; she may not be able to do this and may feel guilty if she gets hurt and does not tell you. She needs to hear that it is the adult's job to notice what is happening and keep her safe, but also get the message that nobody in the family should need to keep secrets.

Role-model this yourself by adopting a 'zero tolerance' attitude to aggression from any of your children, and indeed any family member. Remember to include family pets in this embargo. Children who have sibling rivalry issues may also feel rivalrous towards pets and try to hurt them. In this situation, try to avoid pets being in the same room as the child when you are not there.

Losing Resources and Belongings

👁 OBSERVED BEHAVIOUR

Inability to keep belongings safe.

'Forgetting' to bring homework home or to return it.

😊 ATTACHMENT/ DEVELOPMENTAL TRAUMA ISSUE

Your child may have come from a chaotic household where it was impossible to keep his belongings safe.

He may be losing resources or items of clothing because he carries them around with him and then forgets where he has left them. He may be trying to keep things with him for security – they may remind him of you and these items help him to know that he will be remaining with you. Alternatively, he may have memories of loss and be trying to insure against this happening again.

The child may not feel worthy of having possessions and loses them because they have no value to him.

What can I do?

Support is the key here – your child has missed out on an external modulator. He needs an adult to guide him as one would a toddler. Verbalize understanding of this difficulty: *'I know how hard it is for you to look after your...and to remember to put them away in the correct place. Let's see how we can support you with this.'*

Pin pictures representing the things he needs to have for the various activities in an obvious place.

💥 TRIGGER

Going to and returning home from school.

Visiting friends and relatives.

Taking part in family or individual activities.

Leaving a room or the house.

What can I do?

Provide practical support, such as supplying him with a transparent pencil case with named pencils for school.

Use transparent storage boxes, preferably labelled in a way your child can understand, for example pictorially.

For home and school, use prompt cards, possibly pictorial and laminated, so items can be ticked off each day and for every activity he usually participates in. There could also be a box for ticking the items back in at the end of the activity.

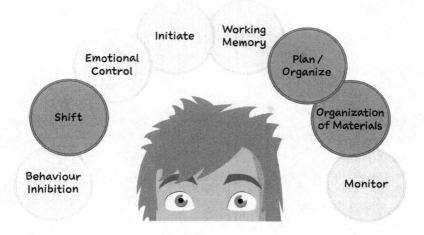

📖 FURTHER REFLECTIONS

Some children have had no guidance as to how to safeguard their personal possessions and will need your help to do this. You need to empathize with his difficulties: *'Nobody taught you this when you were little. Isn't it great you now have me to help you with this?'* Or: *'Let's work together to help you feel good enough about yourself to know you deserve to have nice things.'* Or: *'Why don't you practise leaving this at home for now?'*

If homework is an issue you could ask the school to email you details of your child's homework tasks and return a copy by email to the school. If lack of self-worth is one of the reasons for your child's difficulties, then retuning his homework gives a message that you feel he is worth making an effort for. (NB: Some children are obsessed with keeping their own resources organized and manage this well as they feel it is the only area of their life over which they have full control. As they begin to feel safer, their organization skills may deteriorate. While frustrating, this might actually be a sign of improvement!)

Lying

👁 OBSERVED BEHAVIOUR

Lying.

😊 ATTACHMENT/ DEVELOPMENTAL TRAUMA ISSUE

Survival strategy – she may have been deprived and neglected in her early history. She may have experienced the need to lie in order to keep herself safe.

Fulfilment – she lies to compensate for what she missed in her early life.

Fear – she may have experienced unpleasant reprisals in the past.

Insecurity – your child may be feeling insecure because she is unsure about the permanence of her present placement (regardless of how permanent it actually is) or because of feelings of rejection and shame.

Lying gives her some control and power.

Shame – she believes she is worthless and so acts accordingly.

She is likely to have been lied to by her birth parents, the abuse being reinterpreted as an 'accident' or your child's responsibility.

What can I do?

Discuss, agree and role play alternative strategies for different scenarios.

In role play scenarios, help your child develop a mantra that she could say to herself when she feels she is in a difficult situation: 'Oops, I've done something wrong. I must try not to panic. It will be okay.'

Help your child practise considering whether the events that lead to her lying are really big or small issues.

For shame-filled children, offer support: 'Can I help you feel good enough about yourself to tell the truth?'

💥 TRIGGER

The child may have acted in a manner that she knows is unacceptable and that will have consequences. She lies in an attempt to avoid the consequences of her actions.

Lying might be a 'habit' she has learned.

Your child might also lie because she lacks self-worth – you would not like her if she told the truth.

What can I do?

If you know your child has lied, do not ask her if or why she has. She does not know why, and may feel increased shame that she has not managed again.

Validate your child's feelings: 'I know you struggle to let me know what happened and I guess it's because you were scared about the consequence of what you did.'

Although sanctions need to be relevant to the 'crime', you need to ensure that the sanction does not further shame your child. While your child needs to accept responsibility for her actions and manage the consequences, you may need to support her in this. Short, concise scolding helps to reduce the shame.

Avoid drawn-out investigations if at all possible.

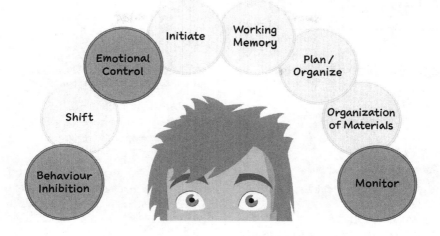

📖 FURTHER REFLECTIONS

Understandably, lying is considered by many to be a serious misdemeanour and it creates anxieties that this will continue into adulthood. Often this can be linked to parents' own belief systems that they learned as children. You may have been taught that lying was terrible and are looking at it from this perspective.

You need to look at it from your child's perspective; i.e. as a survival strategy or as something she learned from the lies of adults around her. Your child cannot help what she is doing and needs the support of all the adults in her life to help her. Being sad for her rather than angry will help her to see your empathy rather than your anger.

This will be easier to manage if you can see your child's lying as a sign that she is not feeling safe.

Some children tell lies almost to get into trouble rather than to get out of trouble. Whatever the circumstances, an empathetic, understanding attitude will work better than a critical one. If you have more than one child and are unsure who is lying, don't get into protracted discussions about who has done what. Instead, act on your gut instinct. You can apologize later if you discover that you've got it wrong. This will not damage your relationship with your children. Instead, you will be able to model making a mistake, apologizing and this not being the end of the world.

Managing Group Settings

👁 OBSERVED BEHAVIOUR

Not leaving a parent's side when in a group setting.

Tantrums.

Requests to go home.

Interrupting conversations.

Fighting with other children.

😊 ATTACHMENT/ DEVELOPMENTAL TRAUMA ISSUE

Insecurity – your child may have suffered several moves in his life; he may have experienced physically being taken away from his known caregiver, or caregivers not returning to collect him.

Fear – your child may have been left with unsafe adults in the past. Although he may trust you in home settings, this trust is dissipated in a group situation.

Control – your child knows that you will be affected by a display of temper at your seeming abandonment of him. However, he is unable to quash this need for control; it's a case of 'can't do' rather than 'won't do'.

It's important to monitor the quiet child who clings to you as he may be struggling with the separation and may be dissociating as a means to protect himself.

What can I do?

Arriving early might help. That way you can help your child prepare for newcomers.

Try cognitive approaches – talk to your child about his worries and concerns before the event and about what you might both do to help.

Don't belittle your child's feelings as his development may be at the level of a toddler and his feelings and reactions are very real to him.

Give your child a task that he can do as this might allow him a feeling of control. Try to make this something that he needs to check in with you about on a regular basis.

💥 TRIGGER

Fear of abandonment.

Struggling to share attention.

Noise.

Reminder of past trauma. The child may have lived in a chaotic environment with people coming and going in a random manner.

What can I do?

Validate his feelings, with empathy: *'I know you struggle when we go to parties. I guess it reminds you of scary times in the past. Maybe it will be easier if you wear this scarf to remind you that you're safe now.'* Or: *'I know it's hard for you to share my attention. How about you practise playing with (another child) for five minutes and I will come and give you a cuddle?'*

You could suggest your child stays close to you and holds your hand while you talk to other people.

Agreeing a time to leave together might help a child recognize that you won't abandon him and will put some parameters around the event.

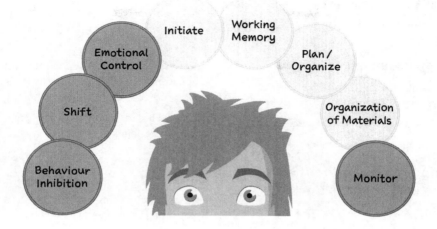

📖 FURTHER REFLECTIONS

It can be very restricting to parent a child who struggles in group settings. Friends and family may find it difficult to understand and your friendship network might be restricted. Talking to family and friends and eliciting their support might help. If there are other children in the group, they could be encouraged to invite your child to play. Preparing your child in advance of any group setting, empathizing with his struggles and agreeing a way to manage these might help. You may want to develop a mantra that you and your child can repeat during the event: '*I am safe, Mum loves me and we are going home together.*'

Try not to become frustrated with your child's difficulties; remember, he is doing the best he can. Arriving early at any group gathering might help, as will knowing the guest list and talking about this with your child in advance. If you feel that the level of noise might be a factor you could agree that your child listens to music on his own device so that he can control this.

Moving On

👁 OBSERVED BEHAVIOUR

Inability to 'move on' from a situation or disappointment.

Feelings of being treated unfairly.

Statements that 'It's unfair'.

😊 ATTACHMENT/ DEVELOPMENTAL TRAUMA ISSUE

Shame – anxiety about being wrong. This child may have been in an environment where she lived in a constant state of fear. She may have been blamed for her own and others' actions. She may feel an over-whelming sense of responsibility for what has happened to her and others close to her and feels easily shamed when something happens that leads to a feeling of failure.

Need for fairness and justice – she may have experienced settings where siblings were treated differently; a need for fair shares could have been a survival strategy, hence her need for fairness in the present.

Disassociation – a memory may have been triggered and the child dissociates in order to cope.

Fear of rejection – she may worry that her actions will cause others to reject her, an experience she may have suffered in her early life.

What can I do?

Validate her feelings: *'I know you find it difficult to forget what has happened, especially if you feel it was unfair. Let's see if I can help you with this.'*

If necessary, give her a few moments with a supporting adult to express her anxieties before she moves on.

If the child is disassociating, place a gentle hand on her shoulder to bring her back to the present.

💥 TRIGGER

A conversation, a perception of injustice, a disappointment, an argument at home.

A feeling that to move on will mean a loss of control.

Fear or anxiety about what will happen next.

A feeling that familiarity may be less frightening, even if this leads to confrontation.

What can I do?

Use a visual and interactive method to help her move on; for example, provide a small, plastic dustbin and some pieces of paper so any issues can be written down and thrown away. Support your child in using this. She may need to talk about her feelings before putting them in the bin.

Provide a book that your child can use to express her emotion and then 'leave it there'.

Provide a routine to distinguish between different activities. A reminder a few minutes before an activity is due to change may help your child to prepare herself for the change.

Recognize her difficulties: *'I know you struggle when you think you are treated unfairly. I can understand why.'*

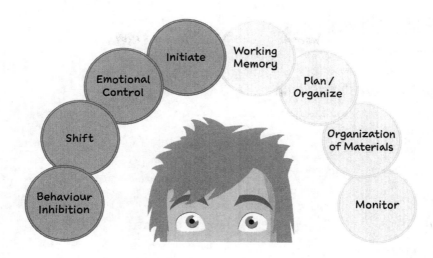

📖 FURTHER REFLECTIONS

Early trauma can mean that getting ready for school and getting out in the morning will be very difficult for your child. She may therefore arrive at school having experienced upset at home and may be feeling responsibility and shame for this. She may be experiencing regret and anxiety which she acts out in anger or dissociation. Empathizing is essential: *'I guess I would struggle to get dressed if I was worried about going to school.'* Constant complaints of unfairness can be draining and frustrating and parents can be caught up in trying to defend their actions and demonstrating why they have been fair.

Since your child's feelings are a reflection of her early trauma history such discussions are largely unproductive. Instead, empathize with the feelings: *'I know it's really hard for you to feel that I treat you fairly. I can understand why. I guess I might feel like that if I had been hurt the way you were when you were in your birth family.'* Or: *'I think you're struggling to know that I can love both you and your sister. Would it help if I gave you a cuddle before you moved on to do...'* You could devise 'moving on' games; for example, Simple Simon Says, move three steps to the right.

Peer Problems

👁 OBSERVED BEHAVIOUR

An inability to relate to peers appropriately.

Unpredictable behaviours that leave peers bewildered and feeling vulnerable.

Controlling behaviours that alienate peers.

Choosing inappropriate friendship groups. Traumatized children tend to drift towards other traumatized and challenging children.

☺ ATTACHMENT/ DEVELOPMENTAL TRAUMA ISSUE

The need for control: your child lost control early in his life; he is not prepared to accept controlling behaviours from others.

Fear of rejection can lead to rejecting behaviour or in contrast, he could be overbearing and overwhelm peers by his constant and demanding attention.

Shame does not allow him to consider himself worthy of friendships.

Your child may have never been taught how to play collaboratively and needs assistance with this.

Your child has experienced difficulties attaching to his primary caregiver because of his early life experiences; secondary attachments need to develop after this.

Traumatized and challenging children tend to gravitate towards other traumatized and challenging children, perhaps because these children reflect their early experiences and thus their inner world.

What can I do?

Supporting your child to manage his impulses and to control his emotions will improve his chances of maintaining firm friendships.

Cognitive strategies and role playing possible incidents can help.

💥 TRIGGER

Everyday scenarios with peers will lead to clashes and disagreements.

Not recognizing that friendship can be shared. Your child may struggle if his chosen 'best' friend pays attention to other children.

Moving from 'best' friend to 'best' friend.

What can I do?

It is incredibly difficult to alleviate peer problems but it is possible to set up groupings to enable more appropriate friendships to be made.

He may only be able to manage limited periods with his peers, and may need short sessions to 'practise' peer relationships. If you think your child might manage 15 minutes of peer time he could play for ten minutes; that way he has an experience of success rather than failure, and you are not waiting until something goes wrong and then stopping play. He is likely to need adults to monitor how he is managing, so it might be better to encourage friends to come to your home rather than him going to theirs.

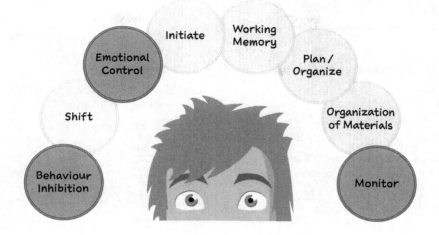

Social integration for your child is important, but may be difficult to achieve. The peers who could become invaluable role models may be concerned about your child's unpredictable behaviours and have higher self-esteem levels that prevent them from falling under his control. (This may lead to your child gravitating towards inappropriate peer relationships.) Other parents may be wary of their child's relationship with your child; they may feel less wary if you develop a relationship with them.

This inability to keep friends or have inappropriate friendships can be particularly upsetting for parents and the idea that your child may be experiencing loneliness or rejection can be especially painful. Try to remind yourself that your child will have the opportunity to manage peer relationships later when he has worked on his emotional control issues and getting some of his 'baby' needs met. At this time, he may need parent time rather than peer time.

Running Away

👁 OBSERVED BEHAVIOUR

Running away from home.

😊 ATTACHMENT/ DEVELOPMENTAL TRAUMA ISSUE

Fear, insecurity, a sense of unworthiness, shame and rejection are all key to this type of behaviour.

The child may feel a need to abandon before being abandoned.

Peer pressure combined with low self-esteem and a need to be accepted might also be factors.

What can I do?

Validate your child's concern. It is crucial to keep calm. If your child has a history of absconding, she may need to be closely supervised.

Your child needs to know that the adults in her life can keep her safe. She needs to understand that interventions to prevent her from absconding are measures to keep her safe rather than a punishment.

If a group of peers are absconding together, police involvement may be necessary.

Providing a photograph or item from home can give reassurance and can serve as a reminder that you are there for her when she returns.

⚡ TRIGGER

A particular incident or anticipated activity triggering feelings from the past.

Not wanting to hear what a parent is saying.

Fear of abandonment.

A need to check that you care enough to look for her.

Feeling that she can't do anything right; low self-esteem.

What can I do?

Discuss the underlying reasons for her difficulties at a time when she is calm to help her understand and appreciate adult concerns regarding her vulnerability and safety.

Look for triggers and empathetically acknowledge these.

Provide alternative strategies for her when she feels anxious or threatened, for example allow her the possibility of going into the garden or her room.

Role play scenarios so that these strategies can become embedded.

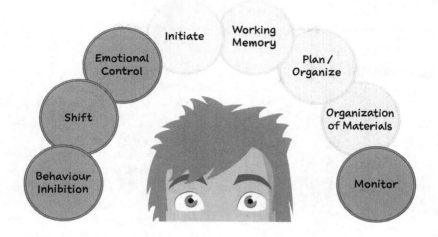

📖 FURTHER REFLECTIONS

The level of vulnerability will dictate the prevention and management of this behaviour. Safety has to be the primary concern, especially in light of the vulnerability of these youngsters. However, if your child is also aggressive, leaving the house for a short period may be a better alternative to angry outbursts where others are put at risk. The key is to work with your child to give her the message that you can help her manage her feelings and behaviours. Helping your child to recognize that her behaviour may emanate from her past might help her to recognize that you will not abandon her: *'I guess I would find it difficult to believe my mum would be there for me if I had been let down in the way you have. If I had these feelings I guess I would like to run away from them.'* Try to identify triggers and talk to your child about these when she is calm: *'I've noticed that you often run away when you've had a tricky day at school. Do you know I love you even when you've been struggling in school?'*

You could suggest running away with her or agreeing a 'running away venue' or a 'running away time'. This could be agreed on the basis that, if your worries are lessened, you won't need to report her missing.

Offering a 'running away goody bag' with snacks might demonstrate that you care about her health and safety. Here the 'trick' is to offer the goody bag with humour and empathy. This is not likely to increase her running away; instead, it might reduce it as your concern will counteract the abandonment fears that are the underlying reasons for the behaviour. If you need to talk about a difficult subject, set this up in advance: *'I know you're going to find this discussion hard and I guess you might want to run away. However, I do need to talk to you about... Maybe we can agree on a five-minute discussion and see how that feels?'* Playing games like 'hide 'n seek' might help. Role play how you manage angry feelings. For example, talk about how frustrated you felt when your washing machine broke down and how you really wanted to run out of the house to get away from the washing but that on reflection you decided to go into the garden and have a good scream instead.

School and Separation Issues

👁 OBSERVED BEHAVIOUR

Screaming and acting out, crying quietly or dissociating when leaving for school or other activity.

'Losing' shoes, coats and so on.

Refusing to put on outdoor clothing.

Using 'slow down' actions to avoid leaving.

😊 ATTACHMENT/ DEVELOPMENTAL TRAUMA ISSUE

Insecurity – your child may have suffered several moves in his life; he may have experienced physically being taken away from his known caregiver or his caregivers not returning to collect him.

Fear – your child may have been left with unsafe adults in the past. Although he may trust you, the separation can still raise unpleasant memories.

Control – your child knows that you will be affected by a display of temper at your seeming abandonment of him. However, your child is unable to quash this need for control; it's a case of 'can't do' rather than 'won't do'.

It's important to monitor the quiet, seemingly non-responsive child as he may be struggling with the separation but may be dissociating as a means to protect himself.

What can I do?

An effective intervention is to work with the teacher to bring your child in a little earlier than the rest of the class. This enables more time to focus on and settle your child.

Cognitive approaches, possibly using metaphor and role play can assist behaviour inhibition.

It is important not to belittle your child's feelings as his development may be at the level of a toddler and his feelings and reactions are very real to him.

At the end of the day, remind your child of earlier feelings and that you are here: *'This morning you were upset when you left me. But I'm here to collect you. I missed you today and want to hear what you did. I wonder if you'll be so upset tomorrow.'*

💥 TRIGGER

Leaving the caregiver.

Fear of abandonment.

What can I do?

Validation of his feelings, with empathy: *'I expect you're a bit frightened that I won't come back for you. That must be really hard. I will be back this afternoon, after story time'* (or whatever you know your child will be doing last thing). Or: *'I guess you're really cross with me leaving you. I wonder if that's because you're not sure if I really love you when I leave you with other people. Here is a photograph/ token/toy to help you with these feelings.'*

Put notes in your child's lunch pack with messages that you are missing him and looking forward to seeing him.

Give the teacher a little toy or card from home ready for occasions when your child is struggling.

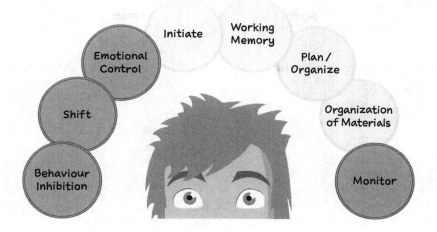

📖 FURTHER REFLECTIONS

It can be upsetting to leave a child who is upset; however, most quickly settle. You may want to develop a leaving mantra which you can say to the child when you leave and that the teacher can reiterate during the day: *'I hope you have a good day; I'm really looking forward to hearing all about it when I collect you.'* Or: *'I know you'll miss me; thanks for letting me know this. I will also miss you and think about you during the day. I will see you at 3 o'clock.'*

Try not to become frustrated when your child can't find clothes, shoes and so on. Have a spare set you can produce when your child 'loses' his clothes.

Use humour to manage 'slow down' actions. You could suggest a slow dressing competition when it's not vital for you to get out at a certain time. You could thank your child because that gives you a chance for another cup of tea and hope he has worked out what to say to the teacher when he gets to school.

If you are more anxious about time keeping than your child, this will make it more likely that he will 'use' losing clothes or 'slow downs' as a control mechanism. You may have to work with your child's teacher to ensure that there is an agreed way to manage any latecoming so that this is not shaming for your child and you are not left feeling like a 'bad' parent. It's your job to support your child to get to school but it's not a sign of being a 'bad' parent if your child still struggles to leave home. Helping him with his feelings of abandonment are more important than time keeping.

Self-Harming

👁 OBSERVED BEHAVIOUR

Self-harming can range from extreme behaviours like cutting arms to more, seemingly, minor behaviours like scratching skin, biting the inside the mouth, head banging or eating issues.

Self-harming is often felt to be more relevant for older children; however, self-harming behaviour can be seen in babies and toddlers.

☺ ATTACHMENT/ DEVELOPMENTAL TRAUMA ISSUE

Shame – your child may feel responsible for what happened to her in the past; she may have been told that it was her fault. She may feel that her actions led to her being taken away or to others being punished. Self-harming allows her to 'punish' herself for this.

Using self-harming to manage emotional pain.

Dissociative children might self-harm to connect with feelings or as a means of getting attention, checking out that her parents care enough to be worried.

What can I do?

Supervision might minimize opportunities for self-harming. However, this will not be effective without addressing the underlying reasons.

Do not ask, 'Why did you do this?' She does not know the answer and she is likely to feel increased shame and therefore increased need to self-harm.

Work with the school so that they can support your child and monitor any incidents of self-harming in the school setting.

💥 TRIGGER

Being reprimanded or expecting to be reprimanded for a misdemeanour.

Any situation that arouses anxiety.

Inner feelings of abandonment or fears that are difficult to identify in specific behaviours.

Being alone – children may engage in self-harming behaviour when they are on their own.

What can I do?

Be sensitive to possible triggers and address these in advance of having to reprimand your child.

Let her know that you love her and that you need to talk about whatever is bothering her.

Pre-empt your child's behaviour by acknowledging and validating her behaviour and emotions: *'I've noticed that you've scratched your arm. I'm wondering why? Are you forgetting that what happened to you in the past wasn't your fault?'* Or: *'I'm wondering if you're forgetting that I love you? Can I help you check that out with a cuddle so that it might be easier for you not to hurt yourself?'*

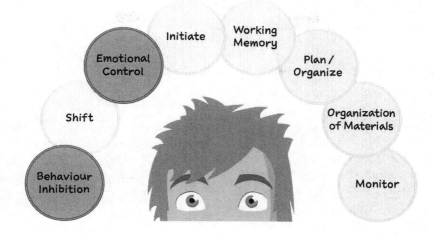

📖 FURTHER REFLECTIONS

Self-harming is a serious issue that needs to be addressed as soon as you notice it. You will need to work hard to recognize the underlying reasons for your child's behaviour and potential triggers. This means knowing as much as possible about your child's early history and how this might have impacted her. You may need help to do this. It's important not to minimize your child's behaviour or the potential implications. Self-harming in a toddler may lead to more extreme behaviour as your child grows into adolescence where she will have to cope with hormonal and developmental issues as well as the impact of her early traumatic history. You need to feel confident about naming the behaviour you see, in a non-shaming way, alongside empathy with why she finds it difficult to keep herself safe.

Talking about this in a supportive way will give your child the message that she does not have to manage this on her own. It also provides the message that the behaviour and underlying reasons are not so overwhelming that self-harming is inevitable. This may go some way to helping your child get some sense of mastery over the inner feelings that are overwhelming her. Offering alternatives, such as seeking you out for a cuddle, might help. But you may have to be proactive in noticing when your child is struggling and be prepared to offer her attention. Transitional objects can be used to help your child know how much she is loved when you are not there; for example, when she is at school or at night time when she is in bed alone. You may need outside support to address self-harming issues. This might include referring your child for therapy. However, you need to be sure that the therapy is one that meets her needs. Non-directive play therapy may not be appropriate, especially if you are not directly involved in the work.

Sexualized Behaviour

👁 OBSERVED BEHAVIOUR

Sexualized language, gestures, play.

Sexual exhibitionism, masturbation or sexualized behaviour towards self or others.

☺ ATTACHMENT/ DEVELOPMENTAL TRAUMA ISSUE

Your child may well have been subjected to, or witnessed, some form of sexual abuse, or lived in a home where inappropriate sexual language or behaviour took place.

He may equate sexual behaviour with demonstrations of affection due to messages he was given by his birth family.

He may use this behaviour to self-soothe.

He may have mixed feelings about sexualized behaviour. He may know that you do not approve of it and feel guilty, yet also gain pleasure from it.

What can I do?

Put practical measures in place to prevent risk to siblings; your children should be carefully monitored and should not spend time together unsupervised.

Use monitors in bedrooms to help you keep your children safe.

Discuss with your child's teacher how to protect your child and other children and also to consider teaching situations, for example sex education lessons, that might affect your child.

☀ TRIGGER

Triggers are likely to be unknown, even to the child.

It could be an occasion when the child feels threatened, unsafe or feels the need to be in control.

Unmonitored internet access.

Time spent with a sibling without adult supervision.

What can I do?

Provide support with controlling impulses in general.

Use preventative and practical interventions. Having rules about not being in each other's rooms or minimizing occasions when children play together will reduce the opportunity for children to act out in a sexually inappropriate way. Your child needs to know not only which behaviour is not acceptable but also what is: *'I noticed that you (touched…in a sexual way/name the behaviour). That is not okay; you can hold her hand but only if she agrees and when there is an adult there.'*

Have a house rule that there are no secret behaviours in your house.

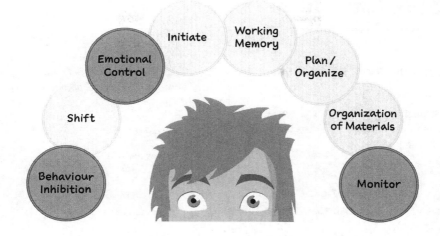

📖 FURTHER REFLECTIONS

Sexualized behaviour is a worry for all concerned and often constitutes a child protection issue; schools are legally obliged to report incidents that cause them concern.

If you know your child's early life history, it's a good idea to share this with the school. You should also share any sexually acting-out behaviours you have observed and discuss ways of managing this in school. The safety of your child and other children is paramount and this needs to be part of the discussion. In order to provide safety, to protect yourself and to protect against allegations, you need to ensure that you are not placed in vulnerable situations. Help your child practise being with you in a non-sexualized way by naming the inappropriate behaviour and also an alternative: *'You learned to touch adults/your sister in a sex way that is not healthy. I need to let you know that it's not okay to touch my breasts. Why don't we practise sitting together holding hands. That is a good way for adults and children to feel close.'* Or: *'It's my job to show you how you can be close in a safe way. Whenever I see you behaving in a way that is not safe I will let you know and I will let you know what you can do instead.'* Or: *'I will help you be with your sister in a safe way. Meanwhile, it's not safe for you to be with her when I'm not around, so playing in bedrooms is not okay. I've put monitors in the rooms just in case you forget.'*

You may need to address your own feelings about sexualized behaviour in your child so that you can talk to him in a non-shaming and empathetic way. This may mean thinking about how sex education was dealt with in your family and the messages you were given about this. You might struggle more with the idea that your child enjoys sexual acting-out as this does not cohere with your feelings about the 'innocence' of childhood.

Shouting Out

👁 OBSERVED BEHAVIOUR

Shouting out inappropriately.

Struggling to watch TV without either a 'running commentary' or disrupting others watching.

Not allowing siblings or parents to talk.

☺ ATTACHMENT/ DEVELOPMENTAL TRAUMA ISSUE

Need for control – your child may have unpleasant memories of when others controlled her life. Her need for control is crucial to her.

Shame – she feels an immense sense of shame for what has happened to her and her lack of self-worth leads to a feeling that if you are not paying attention to her, she does not exist for you.

A fear of silence – she could have harrowing memories relating to silent or quiet environments.

Some children use noise to drown out past traumatic memories that threaten to overwhelm them.

Fear that you love her sibling more.

What can I do?

Validate your child's feelings: *'I know you find it hard not to shout out when I'm speaking to dad/my friend/your sister. My guess is that you're worried I've forgotten about you. Here's a picture of us so that you can see I still think about you even when I'm talking to...'*

Superimpose a picture of your child onto a picture of you so she can see you 'hold her in mind' when you are not engaged with

hier: *'I guess I would struggle to feel loved if I'd had lots of awful things happen to me when I was a baby.'*

⚡ TRIGGER

Parents paying attention to a sibling.

Parents talking to each other.

Friends or relatives visiting.

Parents talking on the telephone.

What can I do?

Remind the child before visitors arrive: *'Today we're going to try hard for you to remember that I love you all the time.'* Or: *'Let's practise knowing I can love two children.'*

Use a pre-arranged signal or code-word as a reminder when your child starts to shout out or interfere.

📖 FURTHER REFLECTIONS

Try a 'silent competition' with a prize of a cuddle for the first person who talks and two cuddles for the rest of the family. Suggest five minutes of non-speaking practice and give your child a timer so that she can assess progress. Offer encouragement, even when she 'fails': *'Well done! You managed a whole minute.'* Or: *'Thanks for letting me know you're still struggling with this. I guess I made a mistake and suggested a length of time that was not okay for you.'* Try a 'speaking contest' instead, with the suggestion that your child manages 15 minutes of non-interrupted talking. She is not likely to manage this and you can be surprised and amazed by the results.

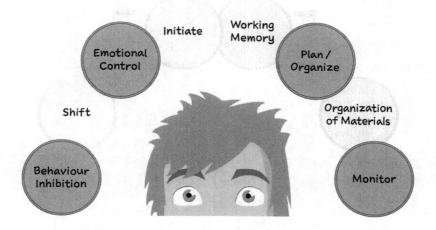

Wonder if she can enter the *Guinness Book of Records* for talking skills. Suggest that she writes down the plot of the TV programme rather than shouts it out. You could offer to help. You might also invite her to let you know what the movie is about before you watch it. These strategies need to be used with empathy and humour.

Siblings are likely to find this child's tendency to speak out annoying and can become resentful and critical. This will add to her deep sense of shame and may exacerbate the behaviour. It may also make it difficult for you to maintain friendships as your friends may struggle to accept your child's behaviour. Talk to your friends and empathize with their feelings while, at the same time, trying to enlist their help. Your friends could offer to join the games mentioned or discuss a previous

conversation when you talked about how much you loved your child and missed her when she was at school. Remaining calm and demonstrating that you care for your child may reduce this behaviour over time. However, you will need to bear your other children's needs in mind and accept their right to be annoyed.

It might be helpful to talk to all the children about this problem '...*had a hard time when he was little and is letting me know this by shouting out. Perhaps quiet times are hard for him. I guess it's hard for you when you want my attention as well. To help every-one in the family I'm going to give everybody 15 minutes of individual time to show that I love each of them and to give you children a chance to practise feeling my love when I'm giving attention to another family member.*'

Stealing

👁 OBSERVED BEHAVIOUR

Stealing:
> often items that are not wanted by your child
>
> even when he could acquire the object by different means
>
> even if he knows that the theft will be discovered.

😊 ATTACHMENT/ DEVELOPMENTAL TRAUMA ISSUE

Survival strategy – your child may have been deprived and neglected in his early history. He may have experienced the need to steal and horde in order to survive.

An inability to cope with boundaries.

An underlying belief that he was 'stolen' from his birth parents.

Insecurity – your child may be feeling insecure because of his perception of the vulnerability of his placement with you or because of his feelings of rejection and shame. Stealing gives him some control and power.

He may be testing you.

What can I do?

Try to minimize your child's opportunity to steal.

Provide more supervision, and ensure that there is no temptation.

Ensure that sanctions are relevant to the crime, but do not further shame your child.

💥 TRIGGER

Seeing an item or knowing of its existence and having the opportunity to steal.

Parents leaving their purse unattended.

Thinking a sibling has something the child wants.

Reinterpreting stealing as 'borrowing'.

What can I do?

If you know your child has stolen, don't ask him if he has or why he has. He does not know why, and is feeling shame that he has not managed again.

Act on your knowledge and say you'll apologize if you're wrong.

Role play scenarios without shaming.

Implement relevant consequences that address the balance within the home.

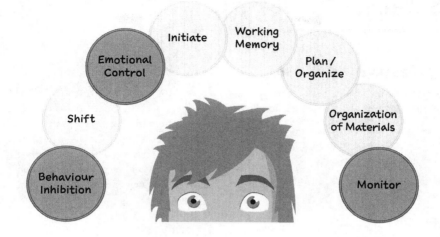

📖 FURTHER REFLECTIONS

Stealing is considered rightly by many to be a serious misdemeanour and it creates anxieties that it will continue into adulthood. Some parents worry that there could be a genetic tendency to crime. However, careful management of the situation can help children through this. Your child cannot help what he is doing and needs the support of all the adults in his life to help him.

Being sad for him rather than angry will help him to see your empathy for him. Anger will only accentuate the immense feeling of shame your child is experiencing. He does, however, need to recognize his responsibility and to experience a consequence for his actions.

If possible, encourage your child to return the item and do something to compensate the victim. This shows other members of the home that stealing is not acceptable but does not shame your child. If money has been stolen and spent, your child could work to repay the money and compensation. If he refuses to do the work, he should repay, with interest, from his pocket money.

If food is being stolen it might be best to supply a small store of food your child can have when he feels empty inside. You might have to provide locks for your other children's rooms and a safe place for your purse. You may have to warn friends that your child has this problem and encourage them to tell you if anything goes missing from their house. It might be best for your child to know this. Explain in a non-shaming way that '...sometimes doesn't feel good about himself and takes things that don't belong to him. You can help him by letting me know if things go missing from your house.' If your child has stolen from a shop, try discussing this with the shop manager before your child returns the goods. You can then agree a way to manage the situation that helps your child.

Stranger Familiarity

👁 OBSERVED BEHAVIOUR

A readiness to trust unknown or unfamiliar adults – no sense of stranger danger.

A tendency or willingness to travel home with other parents or strangers without her parents' permission.

Approaching strangers in parks, shops and so on.

😊 ATTACHMENT/ DEVELOPMENTAL TRAUMA ISSUE

Safety issues – a lack of experience of boundaries, and therefore an inability to perceive danger or the need to keep 'safe'.

Control – a need to demonstrate that she has control over her life.

Rejection – a need to demonstrate to you that she can manage without you.

Retaliation – a need to pay you back for 'leaving' her with other adults during the day.

Adult acceptance – a history of moving from one carer to the next, leading to a general acceptance that she can be cared for by anyone.

Attention – a need for adult attention of any kind.

What can I do?

This child needs the adults in her life to act as her external regulators.

Verbalize the need to be safe and involve her in considering tactics to keep herself safe. Talk through these repeatedly so that she can start internalizing this, perhaps giving her a mantra that she can repeat to herself.

Use photographs of known 'safe' adults and 'strangers' to allow her to practise who she 'knows' is safe. Incorporate some faces that she will recognize (for example, celebrities) but whom it would not be good to go with unless her parents knew.

💥 TRIGGER

Visitors to the home.

Her carer not being there to meet her from school.

Trips to the park, shops and so on.

What can I do?

Your child needs to be kept safe and so the environment needs to be adapted to enable this.

Speak to her about the worry her behaviour causes and the need for you to keep her safe: 'I know that when you were a baby, adults didn't be you safe. As I need to help you learn how to be safe we will practise keeping safe when we go out.' Or: 'We are the adults in your life and we need to keep you safe, so when we go out, you will need to hold my hand all the time.'

Convey that this is not a punishment but a preventative tactic.

Ask your friends to remind her that 'kisses and cuddles are for mum and dad. Let's go and find them.'

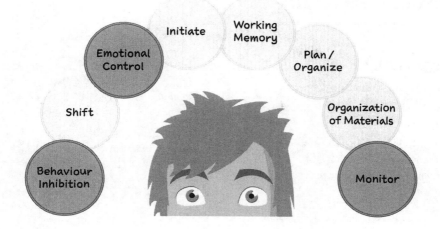

📖 FURTHER REFLECTIONS

Stranger-danger issues can be difficult to manage. Children like these may present child protection issues and in some individual cases, police may need to be involved because of the vulnerability of your child. This is particularly the case if this behaviour is combined with absconding.

In this situation, it is important that you work with authorities to plan a strategy that minimizes the risks to your child. Some adults feel uncomfortable when a child approaches them in an over-friendly way and they withdraw; some adults see it as 'cute' and 'endearing' and will therefore encourage your child. This is likely to confuse your child, as it gives mixed messages.

Some of these children can be very charming to strangers. These situations can be managed by saying: '...is very friendly, isn't she? We're helping her to figure out the important people in her life. I wonder if you could remind her that you are a stranger and she needs to keep her cuddles for mum and dad.' Messages to your child can include: 'I guess you were never shown how special you are and how special mums and dads are. I can help you with this.' Or: 'I know you like to be friendly and helpful but right now you need to stay with me so that we can practise being close.' Home and school need to work together to ensure vulnerable times are covered.

Substitute Teacher/Carer

👁 OBSERVED BEHAVIOUR

Acting out, dissociating or feeling 'ill'.

Overwhelming distress when a parent leaves.

Many children show upset when leaving their carers; for your child these 'usual' feelings can be overwhelming.

☺ ATTACHMENT/ DEVELOPMENTAL TRAUMA ISSUE

Rejection, loss and separation – your child may have real problems making attachments and feel fiercely protective of any positive attachment experiences.

He may have experienced adults disappearing suddenly, not being there when he woke up. He may also have been removed from a placement without warning, or lain alone at night not knowing when adults would return to feed him.

He may have a history of being rejected and expect all adults in his life to fit this pattern. His behaviour is his way of showing his fear and insecurity.

He may fear that parents will not return or that their absence signals a lack of love. He may worry that parents' return will herald abuse (as it did in the past).

What can I do?

If you're leaving your child with a childminder or babysitter, validate your child's feelings. *'I know it's hard for you when dad and I go out. I wonder if you are worried inside about whether you will be safe. I'll give you a picture of us to remind you that we'll be back at...'* Or: *'I know you're upset when I go out. Let's practise remembering that I will be back and that you are safe even if it doesn't feel like that.'*

The morning after you have been out, you might say to him: *'I had a nice time last night but I did miss you. Can we have a cuddle?'*

💥 TRIGGER

Absence of usual teacher.

Change in the person who will collect your child from school.

Taking the child to school or to his childminder.

Parents going for a night out.

What can I do?

Work with the school to help your child.

Find out about any changes of teacher in advance.

Provide a photograph or item from home to help your child manage the day.

Validate his feelings: *'I know you find it really hard when Miss X isn't here to teach you.'* Or: *'I guess you'll struggle to have...collect you from school instead of me.'*

Remember that he might cope better with a familiar teacher rather than a supply teacher, and explain this move as help rather than punishment *'You will feel safer with Mrs Y today as you know her well and you find it hard to focus when you don't know the teacher.'*

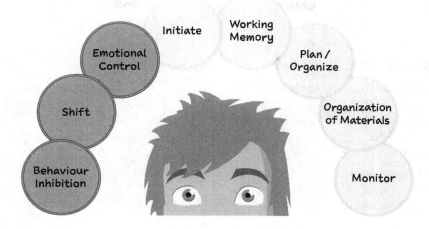

📖 FURTHER REFLECTIONS

Your child's security can be shattered if he walks into the classroom and his usual teacher or teaching assistant is not there. The structure and predictability he craves and needs has disappeared, and he immediately feels insecure and possibly unsafe.

Although many children feel unsettled with a supply teacher, this can be overwhelming for your child and reverberate into a general feeling of unsafety that can make school a scary place. You will need to work with the school so that they understand this and empathize with your child. A photograph of the usual teacher in the classroom may be beneficial.

At home your child is likely to be worried when you are out; and it may be tempting to give up outside activities. However, you do need to help him with these feelings. He needs opportunities to experience your absence and practise managing his feelings about this. The timing of this and ways to manage it need to be considered. You might want start with a very short time out of the house and build up from this. It's important to talk to your child about his feelings both before and after your absence. Reminders of all the times you have come back in the past might help, alongside acknowledgement that it might not feel like that to your child.

Swearing

👁 OBSERVED BEHAVIOUR

Swearing or using offensive language.

This can be in the context of verbally abusing another individual or as an expletive following or accompanying an event or action.

Many children and adults swear in an environment where this is acceptable. Traumatized children don't differentiate.

☺ ATTACHMENT/ DEVELOPMENTAL TRAUMA ISSUE

Control – a perception that the behaviour is unacceptable, with predictable consequences.

Shame – she feels unworthy, therefore acts and speaks accordingly.

Familiarity – a history of acceptance of inappropriate language in her birth home, possibly on an everyday basis, and aimed at the child.

Your child may have experienced or witnessed abusive behaviour and may feel that this language accompanies adrenaline-flowing events or actions.

Lack of boundaries.

What can I do?

Validate your child's feelings: *'I can see you were really furious/worried/ashamed.'* Or: *'I guess you may have learned this language when you were younger. Perhaps I can help you be angry in another way.'* Or: *'I've heard you say...when you... I think this is a word you use when you are excited. Let's think together of a better way to show your excitement.'*

💥 TRIGGER

Another child or adult behaving or speaking in a manner your child perceives as threatening.

An exciting or emotional event.

An attempt to get your attention or your disapproval.

An attempt to shock or control.

What can I do?

If the swearing is linked to retaliation, role play alternative actions. Agree and practise an alternative 'mantra' until this becomes internalized.

If the swearing is linked to actions, agree appropriate expressions.

Reinterpret your child's words: *'Thank you for letting me know you want a cuddle/ love me.'*

📖 FURTHER REFLECTIONS

Your child needs to know that it is unacceptable to use offensive language towards others. However, she may not have been brought up in an environment with these values, or experienced consideration and respect.

She may need help and guidance, just as a toddler is taught within a loving family. There does need to be consequences for swearing. 'Cows' are very loving animals who provide us with the milk we need so you could interpret such descriptions of you as your child saying you are a very caring parent; however, 'cows' can't drive

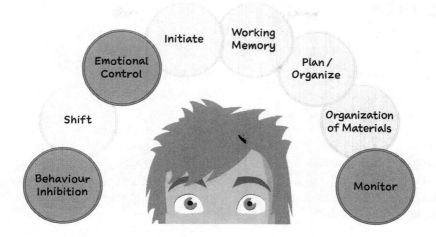

children to fun activities, nor do they have any money for pocket money. It's vital, if you are using this as a learning experience, that you keep ridicule out of your voice and speak in a quiet and calm way.

Quietly speaking your child's language can sometimes help her see the inappropriateness of this language. However, you will need to use this strategy carefully and may need to warn others of your actions in advance and agree their response. You could suggest that she swears for ten minutes and that you will count the number of different words she uses. This strategy needs to be used with humour.

Some children who swear are also aggressive. While neither behaviour is acceptable, aggression is by far the more serious of these behaviours. You may wish to choose your battles, and decide to have a moratorium on swearing while you tackle the more concerning behaviour. In this situation, you need to give a clear message that you don't approve of swearing but that 'for now' you are going to help her to work on her physical aggression and think that she maybe needs to use some swearing as an interim while you work on the main issue. If you are using this strategy, you must feel comfortable with your child's language and be able to praise her when you notice that she has sworn instead of hitting out. You may also need to work with the school on this issue so that they understand your aims and support them if your child swears in front of other children or at the teacher instead of hitting out at another child. Helping other pupils understand why your child is 'getting off' with swearing is important and possible. Children will understand that your child struggles with angry feelings in the same way that other children need extra help with spelling, maths and reading.

Switching Off

👁 OBSERVED BEHAVIOUR

Switching off or dissociating.

This kind of behaviour might be difficult to observe and other people might see your child as being 'the good kid' and having no problems, especially if you also have an acting-out child.

Your child may feel and articulate that he is 'okay', making this harder to manage.

😊 ATTACHMENT/ DEVELOPMENTAL TRAUMA ISSUE

Self-protection – your child may have learned this behaviour at an early age as a means of survival.

The primal and instinctive reactions of 'fight, flight or freeze' may have been the reason your child is still alive.

Control – 'shutting down' feels the only way your child can keep control of his life.

Shame – your child is filled with immense shame about what has happened in the past and this is easily reactivated.

What can I do?

Although your child may not 'act out' and may not be disruptive, provide him with adult support to help him to cope. He needs an external modulator to help him recognize and cope with his emotions, just like a toddler.

Validate his feelings and talk through them.

Support him at the start and end of activities.

☀ TRIGGER

Any challenging situation.

A topic, word, smell, facial expression, body movement, texture, sound, taste or anything that evokes a traumatic memory.

Any situation that arouses anxiety in your child. This could include a situation in which your child feels that he may have been 'bad'.

Your child may dissociate in school and then act out angrily at home.

What can I do?

Your child needs to learn to trust to be able to overcome this primal instinct. This will not be easy and there is no quick fix.

A consistently calm and empathic approach will support him.

He needs to be brought back to the present quietly and unobtrusively so that his shame is not compounded. An agreed code word or signal may help.

Validate his dilemma: 'I can see that sometimes you start thinking about something else. 'Let's see if we can find a way to help you focus.' Also try: 'I can see you are thinking about something sad right now. Would you like me to sit with you?' Or: 'I wonder where you go; perhaps I can go there with you.'

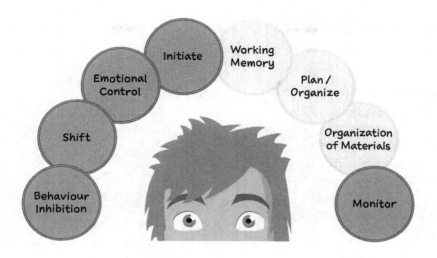

Dissociative children are often considered to be the quiet, 'good' child in a sibling group, especially if they have an acting-out sibling. If you have concerns, it may be difficult to get them validated by other people who feel that your child is managing well.

In this situation, you need to go with your gut feeling in the knowledge that you know your child best. Monitoring your child's behaviour over a period of time may give clues to the triggers causing the dissociation.

If he cannot cope with certain challenges or triggers these may be best avoided if possible, until he begins to feel safe enough to manage these. If these cannot be avoided, it is best to name and identify them in advance and remind your child he is safe now. Gently placing a hand on your child's knee or arm may bring him back to the present; however, you will have to ensure that this does not lead to further traumatization of your child.

At the same time as trying to protect your child, you will need to help him to feel more comfortable in feeling and expressing difficult emotions.

Naming the feelings that underlie the behaviour along with strategies for managing these feelings is essential. Strategies can include offering your child a cuddle before talking about difficult feelings.

A 'switched-off' child may have even more issues than an acting-out child. If he does not get help to address these now, his difficulties may explode during adolescence in self-harming and other worrying behaviours.

Making sure that an acting-out child's needs are not prioritized at the expense of a dissociative child is crucial. He needs as much time and attention even if he does not feel comfortable being in the spotlight.

Talking Constantly

👁 OBSERVED BEHAVIOUR

Talking/shouting, making noises either vocally or with resources at inappropriate times.

Interrupting parents when they are speaking to other people. Humming, singing and so on.

Interfering with parental attempts to engage with siblings.

😊 ATTACHMENT/ DEVELOPMENTAL TRAUMA ISSUE

Need for control – your child may have unpleasant memories of when others controlled her life.

Her need for control is crucial to her.

Shame – she feels an immense sense of shame for what has happened to her.

Lack of self-worth leading to her being unsure how to respond appropriately.

A fear of silence – she could have harrowing memories relating to silent or quiet environments.

A fear of being engulfed with memories and feelings from the past.

What can I do?

Remind the child by a statement before a potentially difficult time: *'Let's practise you knowing that I love you even when I'm talking to/doing...'*

Use a pre-arranged signal or code word as a reminder.

Provide a pictorial reminder of the fact that you can keep your child in mind, such as her photo superimposed on a photo of you.

💥 TRIGGER

Parents talking on the phone.

Attention beign given to others/siblings.

Being asked a question.

Someone making a request.

Bedtime or other quiet periods.

What can I do?

Validate your child's feelings: *'I know you find it hard when I'm speaking on the phone. I wonder if you think I don't love you when I'm talking to/doing...'* Or: *'I guess I would find quiet times hard if I had been hurt the way I know you have.'* Or: *'If I had all these difficult thoughts I guess I would try to drown them out.'* Or: *'Thanks for letting me know you still need help with this.'*

Join in the noise in an amusing (but not shaming) way.

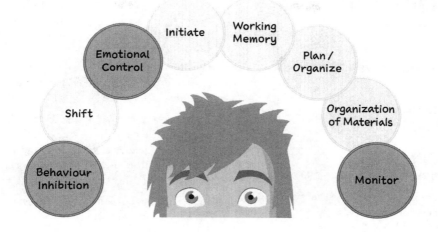

📖 FURTHER REFLECTIONS

Today's environment is busy and often fairly noisy so a silent setting may be a rarity. In the light of this, some form of 'working noise' might be better than silence. You can adjust the type and levels of the 'noise'; for example, soft music (especially Mozart) at home.

Alongside recognizing the reasons for your child's difficulties and empathizing with these, you might also want to provide opportunities to 'practise' quiet times. Games like 'charades' might be fun ways of helping your child. You could also try a 'silent' competition with a 'prize' of a cuddle for the one who talks first. The judicious use of earphones might also help your sanity, although you would need to do this in a way that does not give your child a feeling that you are rejecting her.

If your child struggles at bedtimes you might want to have a pre-prepared recording of you singing that she can put on if she feels afraid of the lack of noise at night.

If your child dominates mealtimes you could try using a timer or other object, maybe a wooden spoon, so that other people get a chance to talk. Each person has an agreed time to be able to talk, or you need to have the wooden spoon to talk. The latter allows for opportunities to share and negotiate. Empathizing with your child about how difficult she might find this will be important. Using humour and recognizing that she might need to practise managing to share will also be important: *'Oops, who has the spoon? I'm wondering how I can help you get the spoon so that I can hear what you want to say?'*

Tantrums

👁 OBSERVED BEHAVIOUR

Acting out.

Tantrums.

Aggression or violence.

☺ ATTACHMENT/ DEVELOPMENTAL TRAUMA ISSUE

The instinctive survival behaviours of fight, flight or freeze. Fighting could have been your child's defence tactic.

Insecurity – your child has not established or internalized a sense of safety, possibly due to his earlier experiences of unsafe surroundings and adults.

Shame – he lives under the shadow of shame.

He feels he is 'rubbish' and so acts accordingly.

Control – a need to have control over others, either by violence or by exhibiting behaviours that cannot be controlled by others.

Fear is often triggered by something in the present that reminds your child of past traumas.

What can I do?

Intervention is better than addressing the behaviour afterwards.

Your child might manage better if he knows what is to happen during the day, so provide a daily programme, displayed in a prominent place.

Allow him to leave the room at the first sign of temper, providing a safe haven, preferably with an adult close by so he feels safe.

Try role play scenarios and cognitive anger-management techniques, helping him to recognize the signs that lead to tantrums and suggesting alternative ways to demonstrate anger or fear.

Support him in repeating a mantra to himself to help him to cope.

⚡ TRIGGER

Disappointment.

A perception of unfairness.

A challenging or shaming situation.

A feeling of fear or being threatened.

Feeling a failure.

Possibly a topic, word, smell, facial expression, body movement, texture, sound, taste that evokes a memory.

What can I do?

Monitor possible volatile settings with a view to intervening before the situation develops.

Validate your child's feelings: *'I know you are very angry. I know you panic when you think you can't manage...'*

Help your child feel he can succeed. You can help him recognize situations where he will struggle: *'We are going to tidy your room and I know that makes you angry. Can I help you with these feelings before we start tidying your room?'*

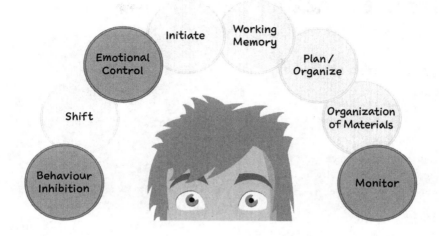

📖 FURTHER REFLECTIONS

Often parents of younger children are told that their child's behaviour is 'normal' and it is just the 'terrible twos'.

If you feel that your child's behaviour is more extreme than this, then go with your gut feeling and address the issue. Your child needs to develop emotional control and a feeling of safety to grow and develop. He needs your help to do this.

The sooner you begin the better; it's easier to tackle tantrums with a four-year-old than it is to deal with an aggressive teenager. An older child may have the emotional age of a toddler. As such, he needs an external regulator to act as a role model to guide and support him. Although you need to keep yourself and other family members safe, 'time out' acts as another rejection. You therefore need to work out a plan in advance to manage your child's behaviour and your response.

Letting your child know what to expect in advance should reduce feelings of rejection and also give him the clear message that you can handle his behaviour. This is crucial as your child feels out of control and uncontrollable.

Your child needs to experience adults being in loving control. Try to create win–win situations: '*I guess…will make you angry.*' If your child becomes angry you can thank him for letting you know that you are getting to know him so well; if he doesn't become angry you can congratulate him on feeling safe enough to handle the situation, then wonder how he will manage tomorrow (don't suggest that managing today means he should manage tomorrow as this sets up a potentially confrontational situation).

Trouble Starting Tasks

👁 OBSERVED BEHAVIOUR

Unable to perform simple tasks including:
- tidying bedroom
- setting the table
- hanging up clothes.

Your child might have been able to complete these tasks yesterday but not today, which is frustrating.

😊 ATTACHMENT/ DEVELOPMENTAL TRAUMA ISSUE

Need for control – your child may have unpleasant (unconscious) memories of when others controlled her life. Her need for control feels crucial and she feels that completing the task would put you in control.

She might have been promised or given things that were removed randomly; perhaps food was used as a weapon of control.

She feels immense shame for what has happened to her in the past and her lack of self-worth means that she is scared to start a task in case she makes a mistake.

Getting things right may not 'fit' with how she sees herself; i.e. 'the bad kid'. This may also make her wary of starting a task.

Triggers may be difficult to identify and may relate to internal rather than external factors. We all have 'bad hair days'.

What can I do?

Remind with a statement before the task: *'I know you sometimes struggle with this. Let me know if you have any questions or if I can help you.'*

Provide a photographic plan of how the task can be done. Try to get your child to help create the plan.

Use a mantra to remind the child of the task.

💥 TRIGGER

Fear of being reprimanded for being slow or not getting the task completed.

Competitiveness

Not feeling good enough about herself to 'get it right'.

Being triggered into a trauma reaction and literally unable to think about what you're asking her to do.

What can I do?

Validate your child's feelings: *'I can see how hard this is for you today. Would you like some help to tidy your room?'*

Remember that for a child who is easily shamed, criticism may add to her shame. Criticism may also confirm your child's view of herself as lacking worth. It may help if you remind her that she is loved however she manages the task you have set her.

Think about what her difficulties are telling you and express this to her: *'I'm wondering if you're feeling worried or anxious about anything?'*

To reduce frustration, remind yourself that this is about how your child is feeling.

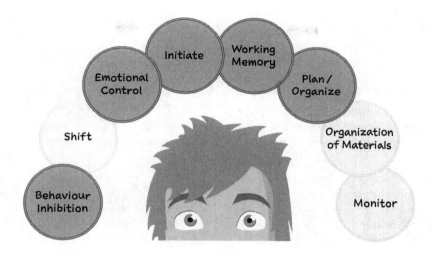

📖 FURTHER REFLECTIONS

You may have to consider your child's emotional age rather than her chronological age when deciding the tasks she can manage; be prepared to help your child as you would a younger child. Remember to offer praise for aspects of the task she manages if she does not complete the entire task; and then suggest ways she might manage those aspects she has not done. Praise should be specific, bearing in mind that your child might struggle with praise due to feelings of a lack of self-worth.

Being prepared to help your child works wonders: *'How about I make the bed while you put your toys away?'* You might need to work on expressing pleasure in being able to help. You might want to suggest your child helps you complete some of your tasks as a trade-off.

Your child could freeze when she goes into her room and can't think how to begin to tidy it; this is a fear response. She could have hyperactive tendencies that will limit her ability to stop and think how to begin tasks or that mean she rushes through them. She might need you to help her think about the beginning, middle and end of the task. Whatever you do, an empathetic approach will be more effective than a demanding one.

Untidiness

👁 OBSERVED BEHAVIOUR

Your child's room is continually messy, filled with scrappy papers, left-over food, dirty clothes and so on.

Your child is reluctant to clean it and seems to feel uncomfortable when you do. It soon reverts to the previous untidy state.

😊 ATTACHMENT/ DEVELOPMENTAL TRAUMA ISSUE

Your child may have started life in chaotic surroundings and has an in-built need to replicate that.

He may feel the need to hoard food as a learned survival strategy. He may not have received adequate food when young or may have needed to fight for it. The food could be there as he has food issues.

Homework may be 'hidden' within the mess as he was unable to focus on this and it remains unfinished; this could lead to difficulties in school.

Control issues – he feels the need to be in control of his own space, although the state of his room is perceived as uncontrolled by the adults around him.

What can I do?

Your child will need ongoing support with this. He will need specific instructions, such as: *'Let's clear out the smelly food first.'* Provide a waste bin.

Demonstrate how to make a bed, fold clothes and so on.

Coach how to put clothes away so that they can be found next time he needs them.

Allocate specified time for organizing rooms, perhaps timetabling a weekly room cleaning time.

⚡ TRIGGER

Being asked to tidy up or thinking you will not notice if the items are under the bed and not in view.

Not feeling good about himself.

Underlying fears that there will not be enough food or love and that he needs to hoard to compensate.

What can I do?

Avoid reprimanding for disorganization, and avoid shaming in front of siblings.

Apply very carefully chosen humour to lighten the situation.

Verbalize your understanding: *'I know you find this really hard.'*

Provide support for your child. He might be overwhelmed by the task of tidying his room. Working together on this might help.

Reflect on what is going on inside for him: *'I wonder if you're letting me know you don't feel safe/good about yourself.'*

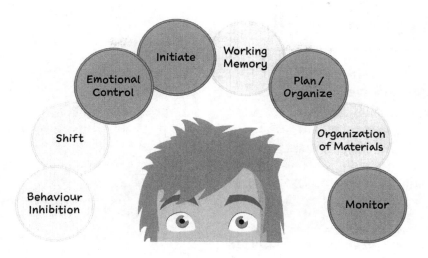

📖 FURTHER REFLECTIONS

Food issues are included here as food invariably ends up in the room! Food issues are often well established and need a careful approach for children who have experienced neglect or abuse. Your child might need a reminder that he now has plenty of food and does not need to hoard it. He may benefit by being given a pictorial representation of how to tidy his room. Take a photograph of the untidy room, then one with the food tidied away, then one with the clothes tidied away. Try to involve your child in taking the photographs as this will give him a sense of ownership of the process. It would be best to laminate the finished product. Your child can use his photographic programme to help him know what to do; he may need adult support to do this.

If the untidy room is a reflection of how he feels about himself, you may need to work on issues of self-esteem and give him the message: *'Won't it be great when you feel good enough about yourself to have a tidy room.'* Older children may benefit from experiencing consequences of their behaviour. If your child does not tidy his room by an agreed day you might want to do this for him; he pays you for the work involved since this is a real-life consequence. It is important that you are 'pleased' about the money you've earned and spend it in a way that he can see and that gives you pleasure. Perhaps you can then wonder if you will get the chance to buy flowers next week. You may choose to do a room tidy to *'let you know how much I love you'*.

Working in Silence

👁 OBSERVED BEHAVIOUR

Possibly disruptive – seemingly an inability to keep quiet.

Dissociates, no longer focusing on the task in hand.

Disrupting parents when they try to have a conversation.

😊 ATTACHMENT/ DEVELOPMENTAL TRAUMA ISSUE

Silence could bring back harrowing memories of unpleasant things in the birth family that took place when the house was quiet.

Silence could enable memories and worries to surface – your child needs to keep talking to disallow any unwanted thoughts to enter her head.

Conversely, she may be consumed by these thoughts and therefore unable to focus.

She may feel threatened when parents are talking together.

What can I do?

Having validated your child's feelings, suggest she practises being quiet for a short period.

Take this very slowly so that she experiences success. Make the expected time clear and do not be tempted to increase it rapidly because she is managing well – stick to the intended plan. If she does not manage, re-adjust your expectation: *'I can see you are having trouble managing five minutes. That's okay. We'll try three minutes tomorrow.'*

💥 TRIGGER

Asked to work in silence or an occasion naturally arises when the family wants peace, for example watching TV.

Parent returning from work.

Parents talking together.

What can I do?

Validate your child's feelings: *'I know that silence is very difficult for you. I guess it might remind you of difficult times in your birth family.'*

Suggest your child sings as she works or plays; sing with her.

Play games that involve silence, such as Sleeping Lions.

Consider having some background music at home. Mozart is especially good.

Give your child an alternative to noise; a quiet toy that she can squeeze.

Have a silence competition with a prize for the winner.

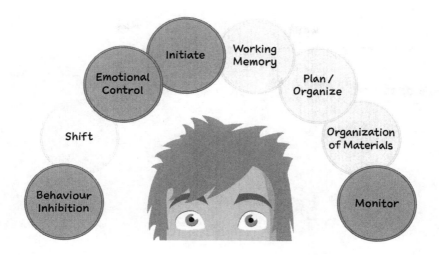

📖 **FURTHER REFLECTIONS**

Start the morning with music to alleviate the need for your child to wake to silence. This might start the day on a more positive note and help your child to feel relaxed. If you have a sibling group, you need to try to make space for all of your children. A noisy child might drown out the needs of a quieter and less demanding child. Empathize with your noisy child about how difficult he finds it when you have time with his sibling; but ensure that sibling time is protected even if this means separate activities at times.

If your child has difficulty managing to keep quiet in class, work with her teacher on strategies that might help her. You might consider giving your child a token from home to help her remember she will be coming home. If this helps her feel safer, it might reduce her need for constant noise. Checking with the teacher how your child has managed will give you a chance to congratulate her on any successes she has had.

Blank Template

👁 **OBSERVED BEHAVIOUR**

💥 **TRIGGER**

😊 **ATTACHMENT/**
DEVELOPMENTAL TRAUMA ISSUE

What can I do?

What can I do?

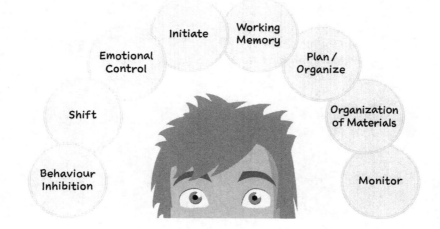

📖 FURTHER REFLECTIONS

Further Resources

ADAPT Scotland is an organization that offers bespoke parenting and therapeutic support programmes to adoptive and foster parents who are caring for traumatized children.

The website provides many free articles and podcasts: www.adaptscotland.org/resources.html.

Check out:
Think Toddler – article by Caroline Archer
The Signs of Secondary Trauma in Parents and Carers – article by Christine Gordon
Violent and aggressive children: caring for those who care – audio interview with Christine Gordon and Karen Wallace

Scottish Attachment In Action (SAIA) is a national charity committed to promoting better experiences of attachment in the Scottish population, in order to effect positive changes in policy and practice in education, care and health. The website includes a wealth of resources, including details of training events, the latest research in attachment and free printable posters for parents: www.saia.org.uk/resources.html

Check out:

How early years trauma affects the brain: the child who mistrusts good care – video of Dan Hughes

Words of Encouragement for Children who have Experienced Trauma – poster by ADAPT Scotland

My Calming Poster - poster by ADAPT Scotland

CairnsMoir Connections is specialist book supplier for those living or working with children impacted by trauma. It provides conference and event bookstalls, online sales and resource signposting, importing the best international publications and highlighting the latest research in child development, therapeutic interventions and training opportunities across the UK: www.cairnsmoirconnections.org.

Check out:

Blame my brain/Know your brain/The Teenage Guide to Stress – Nicola Morgan

The Body Keeps the Score – Bessel van der Kolk

Creating Loving Attachments – Kim S. Golding and Daniel A. Hughes

The Neurobiology of Attachment-Focused Therapy – Jonathan Baylin and Daniel A. Hughes

Reparenting the Child Who Hurts – Christine Gordon and Caroline Archer

The Teacher's Introduction to Attachment – Nicola Marshall

The Whole Brain Child Workbook – Daniel Siegel and Tina Payne Bryson